# Disappointment

## A Subtle Path Away From Christ

Kristi Walker

Learn more about this book
and its author by visiting our web site:
www.overboardministries.com


ISBN-10: 1943635005
ISBN-13: 978-1-943635-00-9



All comments or requests for information should be sent to:
overboard@overboardministries.com

# DEDICATION

This book is dedicated to my grandmothers, Louise Walker and Helen Bartling, both of whom endured tragic loss and disappointment and never ceased to live for God. I would not be who I am today without my spiritual heritage and their love.

To my parents, thank you for continuing their godly legacy.

I am blessed beyond measure.

# CONTENTS

# FOREWORD

Disappointment and discouragement can ravage our souls to the core of who we are. It can unhinge our faith, steal our reason for living, and suffocate our energy and determination to continue.

But it also comes to us as an awful gift, a clarifying tool the Surgeon employs to ply open and dig into the recesses of our hearts... the parts that we ourselves do not even understand. This is when suffering turns into a grace.

Here our disappointment mercifully exposes where we place our confidence and trust. It shines harsh light on what we cling to most for satisfaction and fulfillment. The true gods we worship come to light. We are given a divine moment to see into these self-constructed shrines. The Holy Spirit moves with fire, as Elijah's God did when the prophets of Baal were shown their pitiful worth and powerless god on Mt. Carmel. He painfully, achingly cuts open our hearts and reveals our true idols: idols of self-righteousness, comfort or convenience, of a need for control or power, of a need for the validation of our worth apart from God.

In these severe moments, He lovingly - as only a tender Father, a wounded Redeemer, a skilled Surgeon can - takes the face of our hearts in his nail-pierced hands and lifts our chins and our eyes to meet His. Do we dare look, for fear that our own rebelliousness or self-righteousness will be revealed? Do we allow our guilt and shame, our anger to weigh our gaze downward to the ground?

But once we look—if we look—we will not find harsh condemnation but an overwhelming love. Will it come immediately with a flood, warming our hearts? It may. Or it may only overtake us as we wrestle with it in the night, in the darkness, in the loneliness. But it—and He—will *not* leave.

The Surgeon who plies our hearts was the same one who wrestled with the darkness of his own Father's abandonment. He was left so we may never be left. He was struck down to the grave so we may never be held hostage in the grave.

In the end, Christ's love wins. This isn't about you and it certainly isn't about me. It is about HIM. And if we dare lift our eyes from the rubble and ruin of this world to His, we will not be left wanting. It may be a struggle, an intense grappling match, as His grace reveals more of our soul's selfish clutch to what Elisabeth Elliot called "smashed dandelions."

The healing balm for what disappoints and discourages our souls is found as we drop to our knees in humility and lift our eyes to our Savior, our Redeemer - who does not waste one tear, one hunger pang, one bleeding piece of a broken heart - but redeems them fully for His Glory. There is no other person, religion, relationship, cause, or country who can promise and fulfill this. It is as Hebrews 6:19 says: the Hope for which our soul is anchored.

So go on, lift your eyes.
Be amazed.

Sara Zebulske Bledsoe
Wife of Arkansas Surgeon General and mother of three

# ACKNOWLEDGEMENTS

Special thanks to:

- My dad, Mel Walker, for his inspiration and guidance as a writer;
- My mom, Peggy Walker, for her constant encouragement;
- Pastor Mark Tobey for taking the time to read the book and give advice;
- Kathy Compton for pre-editing the book;
- Overboard Ministries & Joe Castaneda for taking on this project;
- Sara Zebulske Bledsoe, Crista Ashworth, Mindy Stein & Melody Francis King for their contributions;
- Sharilyn Stachler for being a kind, patient and wise editor;
- Alicia Munro for designing the cover;
- All who prayed for me through the process of writing and publication;
- My Heavenly Father for graciously walking with me through life's "disappointments" and helping me to realize that He does not disappoint!

# INTRODUCTION

Awake at 4:00 a.m., I stumbled into the kitchen to find pain relievers. Migraines had plagued me for several nights in a row. Though there was real physical pain, deep inner pain was causing me to ache all over. While I am not a physician, I believe it is very possible that stress or anxiety can cause physical pain. Whether or not that is the case, the deep hurt I felt was the catalyst for writing a book that I know needs to be written—possibly for me more than for anyone else.

Solomon's wisdom certainly surpassed mine, but I possess *some* wisdom from a lifetime of studying the Bible. I have committed hundreds of verses to memory since age two, but the first verse my mom coaxed me to say on audio tape as a toddler is still the answer. It is the answer to the pain I have experienced, and it is the antidote to the topic of this book—*Disappointment: A Subtle Path away from Christ*.

The verse to which I refer is Psalm 23:1: "The Lord is my shepherd I shall not want" (KJV). It is not the only verse in the Bible that we need, but salvation is found there: salvation from despair or the loss of hope. True hope, which is a certainty and not simply a wish for something, fades when we forget that if the Lord is our shepherd, we will lack nothing we need. If it is possible to stay focused on that hope—and Isaiah said it is possible—painful disappointments can be viewed as God's appointments for personal and spiritual growth.

*"You will keep in perfect peace those* ***whose minds are steadfast,*** *because they trust in you"* (Isaiah 26:3).

Presently I reside in Berlin, Germany. Most of Germany's roads are still made of cobblestone, and I say "still made" because they are still making them that way today. Before moving to Berlin I assumed that cobblestone streets were streets from the past, but in Germany cobblestone is being laid somewhere every day. It is kept up stone by stone. The path away from Christ is laid exactly the same way—stone by stone, disappointment by disappointment, until the road is long.

Soon after we come to Christ, we are tempted to wander from Him. Many believers stay focused on Christ and the Word of God and are able, with the power and conviction of the Holy Spirit, to "take captive every thought" and renew their minds. In so doing, we can easily return to the right path before we travel too far. Regardless, the path of following Christ ends up looking something like the veins in a leaf, with the middle vein being our constant walk with Christ and the little veins a picture of our (hopefully brief) wanderings.

A great hymn writer by the name of Robert Robinson once penned these ever-famous and true words:

> *O to grace how great a debtor daily I'm constrained to be!*
> *Let Thy goodness like a fetter bind my wandering heart to Thee:*
> *Prone to wander, Lord, I feel it, prone to leave the God I love;*
> *Here's my heart, O, take and seal it; seal it for Thy courts above.*

In his book, *The Roots of Endurance*, John Piper says,

> *That is my cry: "Let your goodness, O God, bind my heart with a chain to you! Seal my will to yours with an unbreakable application of your eternal covenant." Is this the way Christians should pray? "Keep me! Preserve me! Defeat every rising rebellion! Overcome every niggling doubt! Deliver from every destructive temptation! Nullify every fatal allurement! Expose every demonic deception! Tear down every arrogant argument! Shape me! Incline me! Hold me! Master me! Do whatever you must do to keep me trusting you and fearing you till Jesus comes or calls" (23).*

Instead, in our hearts we often lay a subtle path made up of disappointments that can ultimately lead away from Christ and His goodness, until that path leads to self-destruction. The path you choose to walk will make evident the god you choose to serve. Abide in Christ and your path will lead you to the one and only true God – the God of the Bible, the great Shepherd of our souls. Wander away and lay your own road, disappointment by disappointment, and it will lead you to another master—a master whose supreme specialty is deception.

After all, disappointment is deception, simple and subtle. "It is by our own desires that we are dragged away and enticed" (James 1:14), but we rarely feel we are being dragged away. Certainly, desire is not sin, nor is disappointment. We are simply attempting to live for God's desires and our own at the same time. What is so wrong with that? "Then, after desire has conceived, it gives birth to sin; and sin, when it is full-grown, gives birth to death" (James 1:15). It is inconspicuously happening to people all around us and most certainly inside our own hearts if we are not extremely careful. The answer is to hold firm to the end the conviction, confidence, or HOPE we had at first (Hebrews 3:14).

> *The LORD is my shepherd, I lack nothing. He makes me lie down in green pastures, he leads me beside quiet waters, he refreshes my soul. He guides me along the right paths for his name's sake... Surely your goodness and love will follow me all the days of my life, and I will dwell in the house of the LORD forever.*
> Psalm 23:1-3, 6, NIV

What a path to choose! Oh God, may disappointment never lead us from it.

# CHAPTER ONE
# DISAPPOINTMENT

*"Blessed is he who expects nothing,*
*for he shall never be disappointed."*
**Alexander Pope • from a letter to playwright John Gay**

*"The measure of success is how we cope with disappointment."*
**Deborah Moggach • The Best Exotic Marigold Hotel**

*"The only love that won't disappoint you is one that can't change, that can't be lost, that is not based on the ups and downs of life or of how well you live. It is something that not even death can take away from you. God's love is the only thing like that."*
**Timothy Keller • Walking with God through Pain and Suffering**

What represents life's greatest disappointment to you? For some it would mean life-long singleness or barrenness, for others it may mean decades wasted in a job that does not bring fulfillment and joy. Or it may be some other dream that is simply out of reach. Perhaps you have been physically, sexually or emotionally abused and now you feel that your chances of ever being whole and happy have been ripped from you. Maybe life's greatest disappointment for you is health-related: a disability, chronic pain, disease, etc. Disappointment usually involves *not* achieving or acquiring what we believe would make us truly happy.

When my niece, Ellie, was three years old she started exclaiming, "You don't love me!" when she was reprimanded for something or simply did not get her own way. It starts young. How often do we do this as adults, directing it at God? I have doubted God's love for me when I do not get my own way. I hear many others do it too, using slightly more sophisticated phrases like, "I know God loves me, but it doesn't feel like it," and, "It seems like God loves everyone but me, or answers everyone's prayers but mine."

This belief, or assumption, that God might withhold good from us or withhold His love from us is the reason disappointment was described in the introduction as deception. God is not the source of disappointment, nor could He be. It is contrary to His character. He loves with an unconditional, everlasting love and He desires to give us what is good for us, but He will not give it if it is not truly good. We must trust His definition of "good" because His wisdom is infinitely deeper and richer than ours. "Oh, the depth of the riches of the wisdom and knowledge of God! How unsearchable his judgments, and his paths beyond tracing out!" (Romans 11:33). If you do not believe in God, or do not believe He is sovereign over all, then disappointment is simply bad luck or misfortune. If you do believe in a Sovereign God, then disappointment is a feeling experienced by allowing yourself to doubt His goodness.

My first real memories of being disappointed came in childhood. There were tears when my dad left the house to go to work because I was disappointed not to go with him. I remember the sting of what felt like unjust parental discipline. Time after time, my desire to go to McDonald's or Dairy Queen was met with, "No, we don't have the money, so we will eat at home."

How about school? Disappointments abound at school. People you thought were your friends treat you unkindly. Mom makes you wear something you do not want to wear. Teachers are unfair. Kids are mean. School lunch in the cafeteria was almost always a source of disappointment. Only on Fridays, which were pizza days, did the cafeteria meet my expectations.

Sixth grade was a particularly disappointing year. My family had just moved from Iowa to Pennsylvania and sixth grade began in a new state, town, and school. The very first day, as I took my seat in homeroom, a kid pulled my chair out from under me, causing me to fall on the ground in front of all of my new classmates. Later that year I won a small basketball for participating in a school reading program. Proud of this basketball, I took it to school with me one day. During P.E. class, I attempted to see how high the ball would bounce. I miscalculated ever so slightly, and the ball bounced up hard, hit me in the chin and knocked me out.

Disappointments abound in childhood, and sometimes you ARE the disappointment! Because I was above average height, the local community basketball league recruited me to play in sixth grade. Never having played before, the previous experience with a basketball should have clued me in to the fact that I was not an athlete. In the first game, I got confused and scored four points for the other team. My team was disappointed, but I was a hero to the opposing team who won by . . . you guessed it: four points.

The older you get, the harder life gets. The little disappointments of childhood and grade school should prepare us to deal with bigger disappointments later in life. Some of us grow up in loving homes where our parents help us learn to deal with life's ups and downs, and we are consequently able to extract wisdom from the failures and injustices suffered during childhood and early adolescence. Others are beaten down by life's disappointments and their spirits broken because of abuse, neglect, malnourishment, dysfunctional families, broken homes, poverty, and real-life nightmares. "From everyone who has been given much, much will be demanded; and from the one who has been entrusted with much, much more will be asked" (Luke 12:48b). In other words, those of us blessed with lives full of love must share with those who have a deficit, breathing love and Life into them!

Allow me to share with you a blog post about childhood disappointment by my friend Crista Ashworth, another missionary in Berlin. I recently met Crista and her family, including her daughter Claire of whom she writes, at a café shortly after their arrival in Germany.

## CLAIRE'S DISAPPOINTMENT

We try so hard to create the perfect life for our children. We protect them from bumps and bruises as they take their first steps, we help them find activities they can do well, and we steer them away from risky things. But as much as we try to keep them inside our protective bubble, at some point, each child will come face to face with rejection, hurts and disappointments. (Isn't this uplifting? Hang with me for a minute…)

As parents, I think it is so important that we not only protect our kids, but that we learn how to walk with them through life's inevitable struggles. They don't just need a pep talk or a "look on the bright side" when they have been punched in the gut by rejection. They need someone to grab their hands, look them in the eyes and help them take the next steps. Who better to do that for your kids than you?

Our family recently moved from Texas to Germany—a HUGE change! Everything is new and different, including the language, so we are having to be each others' biggest fans right now. Each day has mile-high challenges, and it is easy to feel defeated and rejected by the time you sit down in the evening. But one particular rejection sent my sweet nine-year-old daughter reeling.

Claire has been taking ballet classes since she was three years old, and she loves ballet more than anything else in the world. In her words, "Ballet is my LIFE!" Now that we are in Berlin, we have been looking for a place that she can continue her training, keeping in mind her goal of becoming a professional dancer some day.

Well, there is a prestigious school of ballet in Berlin—and from our research, we decided we should contact them to see if we could get an audition. This is a "professional" school, where the students attend regular classes of math, language and science during the day and are trained in ballet and performing skills in the afternoons six days a week. Students from many different countries attend this program and most of them are boarding students who live in the dorms on campus. Because it is part of the German public school system, this intensive training is tuition-free (they are very big on vocational/professional training here), and therefore highly coveted. Each year more than five hundred applicants audition, but the school only takes about twenty. So, we went into this knowing that the odds were not in our favor. Nevertheless, Claire bravely went into the audition room with a few other girls, wanting to do her best.

After an hour, the director took us into his office and gave us a very succinct "no." He told Claire that she was "too compact" and did not have the right body for ballet. What Claire's little heart heard was that she was fat and not worthy of being trained as a ballerina. It crushed her. We left the building, Claire crying loudly, and walked the four blocks back to the train. I wanted to make it all better. I wanted to laugh it off and joke about what an idiot that guy was. I wanted to help her find her brave face again and soldier on...but she couldn't do any of that. She was hurting from a shot to her heart.

So, what I did instead was wrap my mama arms around her, draw her close and hug her the whole train ride home. I shared her tears, felt her heartache and let her know I understood. And I also bought her a mango smoothie and a slice of apple tart as we laugh-cried some more about the whole thing.

Then, when she could finally look me in the eye, I breathed some life back into her deflated heart: "Claire, it doesn't matter what that man or anybody else says about you. It doesn't matter how many people tell you that you aren't right for something. You are beautiful! You have a beautiful body that was hand crafted by God. GOD! And God put a talent inside you to dance. He doesn't give talents by mistake or with carelessness. What God says about you is what matters. He knows exactly who you are, sweet girl. He says you are wonderful. You are a delight! You are precious and valuable and worthy because He made you, and He lives in you. And I agree with Him—you are such a beautiful, amazing, talented girl! Anyone who can't see that is blind."

After about thirty minutes more of that line of conversation, she looked at me with relief in her big, blue eyes and gave me a great, big smile. This experience was painful for her heart as well as mine. But through it I learned some important steps for walking my child through disappointment. I hope they are helpful as you encounter disappointing roads to walk with your own child.

## WALKING YOUR CHILD THROUGH DISAPPOINTMENT

1. **Draw her close:** Let her know that you are right there with her and she is not expected to deal with the hurt on her own.

2. **Share the hurt:** Really put yourself in her shoes and imagine how you would feel in those circumstances. If you can't relate at all, then try to imagine how your child is feeling.

3. **Don't rush:** Some of the best emotional healing happens when you just sit quietly with your child and hold her. Give her the time she needs to open up about the situation.

4. **Speak life:** Talk directly into that wounded place and fill up her little heart with truth. Tell her who she is—who God says she is. Help her hear God's voice for herself and get her own mental picture of how God sees her.

5. **Help her take a step:** Working through the emotion is important—and so is moving forward away from the situation. Teach your child not to stay hurt by helping her look forward and take a step. Just like a toddler learning to walk, we have to take steps emotionally to learn how to move past the disappointment into something greater.

Since that audition at "the poopy school," or so we have nicknamed it, we have found another ballet school that seems to be a good fit for Claire. The instructors are nice, the students are nice and were not only helpful when we tried a class, but were fun and friendly, too. Something I tell Claire quite frequently about dance is that most of the time when you audition, you get a "no"... but sometimes you get a "yes!" So it goes with life, right? Life tells you NO all the time; but pushing through to your YES makes it all seem worth it. You can help your child learn that a "no" is not the end in the arena of their hopes and dreams. Processing the emotions, validating her identity and pressing forward can propel her into a whole new place of fulfillment and joy.

Has your child experienced a deep disappointment with a dream or a relationship? How have you helped them take the next step towards healing their heart? (Ashworth)

**WHAT IS DISAPPOINTMENT?**

My disappointments do not begin to compare with anyone who has truly suffered, but disappointment is universal. It is common to every single person living on every continent in God's great big world, and comparing disappointments is not really possible. Grace is given to different people in different amounts to deal with different circumstances. There are people in the world suffering through unimaginable hardships who are happier than people who have it all. The point is that we all understand what it feels like.

I started thinking about this word in college after facing my first "real" disappointment. It is an odd word. *Dis-appointment.* The prefix *dis* usually changes a word to mean the opposite, as in: *disapproval, disagree, discontinue.* (A friend once reminded me that it does not work with *discussing.*) Max Lucado writes in his book *Traveling Light* about the pre-fix *dis.* "*Dis* changes everything. With *dis,* 'obey' becomes 'disobey.' 'Respect' is changed to 'disrespect.' 'Regard' is suddenly 'disregard.' What was an 'ability' becomes a 'disability.' 'Engage' is now 'disengage,' and 'grace' is transformed into 'disgrace.' All because of *dis*" (191).

What is the opposite of an appointment? Does it mean you had an appointment and now you do not? That is precisely what it means. The English word *disappoint* comes from the Old French *desapointier,* meaning to remove from office (The American Heritage Dictionary of the English Language). Usually when someone holds an office, they were appointed to that position. To remove someone from office is to dis-appoint them. If someone has been removed from an office they once held, that appointment was not necessarily self-made.

However, and make careful note of this, the *emotion* of disappointment and feeling of despair can only occur because of a mental appointment, expectation, longing, desire, or hope. **The all-important key to remember in understanding disappointment is that the appointment is self-made.** Without the expectation (self-appointment), the loss of a job would only provide a problem to be solved, challenge to be accepted, opportunity for personal growth, or new venture upon which to embark. The person is now suffering, not because of the loss of title or position, but because they expected that title or position to be ongoing, although it was not to be.

The expectation was that the job would last for such and such a time. However, there are no guarantees in life apart from the character, promises and Word of God. No relationship, job, title, state, dream or possession comes with a life-time guarantee. Even things that do come with a lifetime guarantee will eventually fail. Benjamin Franklin expressed it well: "Our new Constitution is now established, and has an appearance that promises permanency; but in this world nothing can be said to be certain, except death and taxes" (qtd. in Benton).

Forbes.com features a list of "15 Useful Items With A Lifetime Warranty" (Barlow). Here are the 15 items:

- The Davek SOLO umbrella ($99)
- Briggs & Riley luggage (one piece $335)
- The Tilley Airflo Hat for men ($79)
- Cutco Cutlery (set of knives, $1,599)
- Rodda Exterior Paint ($56.48/gallon)
- Green Egg Ceramic Grill ($799)
- Peugeot Pepper Mill (can be purchased on Amazon for $67.68)
- RedHead Hunting Socks ($9.99 a pair)
- ThatsaBowl Tupperware ($25.00)
- Pelican Hardware Cases (Pelican 0350 Cube Case, $290.20)
- Craftsman Hand Tools (three-piece set, $49.99)
- Ross Reels Fishing Reels (no price listed)
- Hammacher Schlemmer Products
- Pampered Chef Cookware (5-piece Stainless Cookware Set, $325)

Even if these things do last for a lifetime, they can still be lost, stolen or discontinued. "Be aware," warns Forbes, "that not all lifetime guarantees are equal. Look for the word 'limited' before lifetime warranty, which signals preconditions for qualification. Watch for exceptions that can leach value from the product guarantee, such as required maintenance, mandatory registration, high cost to return, a warranty that degrades over time, and an item with a predetermined, stated lifetime."

The point is that nothing, apart from God, is truly disappointment-free. At a church planting conference I attended in Berlin, keynote speaker Timothy Keller put it this way: "Everybody has to base their life on something, and if it's not God, it's going to disappoint them."

Disappointments begin as desires, and desires are often good. They also often lead to this emotion or feeling of disappointment. First we desire something, and then we somehow switch from wanting it, to expecting it to happen. *The Free Dictionary* defines disappointment this way: "a feeling of dissatisfaction that results when your expectations are not realized."

An expectation, unless it is in a promise of God, is a mental appointment we set for ourselves. Most times, we do not realize we have moved from desire to expectation until the expectation goes unfulfilled. Then we realize it very sharply, very acutely. Sometimes it is acute enough that we feel disappointment physically as well as emotionally. It is often referred to as stress, but stress is not a *biblical* word. "The term 'stress,' as it is currently used, was coined by Hans Selye in 1936, who defined it as 'the non-specific response of the body to any demand for change'" (What Is Stress?).

**Stress** As defined by The American Heritage Dictionary of the English Language, Fourth Edition: "A mentally or emotionally disruptive or upsetting condition occurring in response to adverse external influences and capable of affecting physical health, usually characterized by increased heart rate, a rise in blood pressure, muscular tension, irritability, and depression."

It is so much easier to tell someone that you are "stressed" than to tell them you are worried or anxious or afraid or, worse yet, doubting God's goodness. No one ever says that, but isn't that exactly what we mean? We often live as if the goal of the Christian life is to let everyone think we are doing well spiritually. We are simply combating a little stress; who isn't? No big deal, right? Let me tell you, it is a big deal.

Stress is not necessarily sin. The sin lies in how we deal with the stress and the unfulfilled desires and expectations. Poor Job went through unthinkable stress when God allowed Satan to test his faith. Tragedies and trials are stressful, but those going through them are not necessarily sinning. However, negative circumstances can tempt us to wonder if maybe the source, whom we assume to be God, is not good. Proverbs 19:3 proves it: "When a man's folly brings his way to ruin, his heart rages against the Lord" (ESV). A man's folly is often his self-appointments, or hopes set in something other than God and His will.

We love to blame God for evil. It is never *our* fault; never the result of a sin-sick, fallen world (though the Bible clearly states that God is good, and we are sinful). The next few chapters will explore some common sources of disappointment to see how they lead many of us to wander away from Christ.

**Disappointment** As defined by Kristi: "An unfulfilled self-appointment, expectation, longing, desire, or hope in someone or something other than God and His will, resulting in feelings of loss, sadness, or even depression."

There is still a question begging to be answered: are we not supposed to look forward to or expect anything? Is that really wrong? Here is an amusing quote from one of my favorite books, *Anne of Green Gables*. "Oh, Marilla, looking forward to things is half the pleasure of them," exclaimed Anne. "You mayn't get the things themselves; but nothing can prevent you from having the fun of looking forward to them. Mrs. Lynde says, 'Blessed are they who expect nothing for they shall not be disappointed.' But I think it would be worse to expect nothing than to be disappointed" (Montgomery Ch. 13). Do you agree with Anne?

We have expectations, both conscious and unconscious, from the moment we get up in the morning. We expect our alarm clocks to ring, the lights to brighten, the plumbing to flow, coffee maker to brew, toaster to toast, and those are the small expectations! We also expect good health, nice weather, easy commutes, friendly people, quality customer service, a fulfilling career, a satisfying social life, harmony in relationships with family and, while we are at it, long life for ourselves and everyone else we care about. After all, for Americans, it's right there in The Declaration of Independence: "We hold these truths to be self-evident, that all men are created equal, that they are endowed by their Creator with certain unalienable Rights, that among these are Life, Liberty and the pursuit of Happiness."

**The crucial question is: are your desires simply desires, or are they expectations?** Not sure? You will be able to tell simply by your reaction when they go unfulfilled. Here is a little quiz I am calling "How Do You Respond When?" Answer honestly!

**HOW DO YOU RESPOND WHEN:**

The internet stops working?

peacefully frantically desperately fail to cope

You lose or break your phone?

peacefully frantically desperately fail to cope

The weather is less than desirable?

peacefully frantically desperately fail to cope

A traffic jam causes you to be late?

peacefully frantically desperately fail to cope

A cashier, waiter, or sales clerk is rude?

peacefully frantically desperately fail to cope

Your health (or the health of a loved one) fails?

peacefully frantically desperately fail to cope

A friend betrays you?

peacefully frantically desperately fail to cope

Your job is draining and unfulfilling?

peacefully frantically desperately fail to cope

Your single greatest desire remains unfulfilled?

peacefully frantically desperately fail to cope

A romantic relationship ends tragically?

peacefully frantically desperately fail to cope

A close family member dies?

peacefully frantically desperately fail to cope

If you find yourself responding peacefully, without anxiety, because of your trust and hope in God, you are in a good place! It is possible!

*This is what the Lord says: The man who trusts in mankind, who makes human flesh his strength and turns his heart from the Lord is cursed. He will be like a juniper in the Arabah; he cannot see when good comes but dwells in the parched places in the wilderness, in a salt land where no one lives. The man who trusts in the Lord, whose confidence indeed is the Lord, is blessed. He will be like a tree planted by water: it sends its roots out toward a stream, it doesn't fear when heat comes, and its foliage remains green. It will not worry in a year of drought or cease producing fruit (Jeremiah 17:5-8, HCSB).*

If you trust or hope in anything besides the Lord, you will be "cursed" by disappointment; so focused on your "false hope" that you will not even notice when good things happen. Do you ever feel like you are dwelling in a parched place in the wilderness, in a salt land where no one lives?

In Hebrew, the word *arabah* means wasteland or barren place, and a juniper, or broom, is a desert shrub that commonly grew in such a place (Visual Bible Alive). Jeremiah is comparing a bush found in a desert with a tree planted by water. The man or woman who trusts in the Lord:

- Is blessed
- Is like a tree planted by water (refreshed, nourished, content)
- Experiences **no fear of** heat (trials) **or worry of** drought (deficiency, shortage, lack)—"The LORD is my shepherd, I shall not be in want"
- Remains green and does not cease to produce fruit

Perhaps no passage of Scripture provides a better answer for disappointment, discouragement or even despair. Trust in the Lord! Put your hope in Him!

Before continuing, allow me to define the difference between **true hope** and **false hope**. When the Bible speaks of hope, as in Hebrews 11:1, "Now faith is confidence in what we hope for and assurance about what we do not see," it is referring to true hope. When we use the word hope in everyday terms, as in "I hope I get that job," we are speaking of false hope. False hope very often leads to disappointment. True hope never does.

**TRUE HOPE:** a certainty; absolute confidence in the object of one's expectations

**FALSE HOPE:** an uncertain wish, desire or expectation

Referring back to the question of whether we are like a bush in the desert or a tree planted by water, the Apostle Paul instructs us, "Do not be anxious about anything, but in everything, by prayer and petition, with thanksgiving, present your requests to God" (Philippians 4:6). He penned these words from PRISON—definitely a place in which one would experience anxiety! The promise, then, is that "the peace of God, which transcends all understanding, will guard your hearts and your minds in Christ Jesus" (Philippians 4:7). If life's circumstances are causing anxiety instead of peace, we must remember that the very Word of God lets us know it is possible to have it the other way around, regardless of the magnitude of the disappointment.

> *How are we going to get the life that has no lust, no self-interest, no sensitiveness to pokes, the love that is not provoked, that thinketh no evil, that is always kind? The only way is by allowing not a bit of the old life to be left; but only simple perfect trust in God, such trust that we no longer want God's blessings, but only want Himself. Have we come to the place where God can withdraw His blessings and it does not affect our trust in Him? When once we see God at work, we will never bother our heads about things that happen, because we are actually trusting in our Father in Heaven whom the world cannot see (Chambers 10/23).*

Is it wrong to have expectations? What do *you* think? Perhaps a better way to put it is that expectations are potentially dangerous. I think we can agree at this point that expectations can lead to some serious disappointment, even disappointment with God! If that is the case, we need to take a very introspective look at our desires and ask ourselves, "Is it my will I want, or God's?" As dangerous as it is to have expectations in anything apart from the will of God, it is far more dangerous when expectation is transformed into an egotistic belief that we *deserve* what we expect!

The Bible contains several passages on contentment, two of them found in the very chapter just quoted; but this introduction to disappointment will conclude instead with a somewhat obscure passage from the book of Habakkuk (chapter 3, verses 17 & 18, made popular by Matt Redman's song "Blessed Be Your Name").

**Though the fig tree does not bud**
**and there are no grapes on the vines,**
**though the olive crop fails**
**and the fields produce no food,**
**though there are no sheep in the pen**
**and no cattle in the stalls,**
**yet I will rejoice in the LORD,**
**I will be joyful in God my Savior.**

## DISAPPOINTMENT

Discussion Questions

1. What represents life's greatest disappointment to you?

2. What is disappointment? What did you learn about disappointment from this chapter?

3. What is a disappointment you are currently experiencing or have recently experienced? In other words, is anything causing you to doubt God's love?

4. If you have children, or play a significant role in the life of a child, what do you do to walk them through disappointment?

5. What is your greatest desire at the moment? How are you likely to respond if it goes unfulfilled? Would your response more closely resemble peaceful trust or despair?

6. Would you say that you truly trust God with your deepest desires? If not, take time to pray and ask God to help you learn to trust Him as you continue this study.

# CHAPTER TWO
# MARRIAGE

*"There is no safe investment. To love at all is to be vulnerable. Love anything, and your heart will certainly be wrung and possibly be broken. If you want to make sure of keeping it intact, you must give your heart to no one, not even to an animal. Wrap it carefully round with hobbies and little luxuries; avoid all entanglements; lock it up safe in the casket or coffin of your selfishness. But in that casket - safe, dark, motionless, airless—it will change. It will not be broken; it will become unbreakable, impenetrable, irredeemable. The alternative to tragedy, or at least to the risk of tragedy, is damnation. The only place outside Heaven where you can be perfectly safe from all the dangers and perturbations of love is Hell."*

**C.S. Lewis • The Four Loves**

*"The trouble is not that I am single and likely to stay single, but that I am lonely and likely to stay lonely."*

**Charlotte Brontë**

*"It is better to be single and wish you were married than to be married and wish you were single."*

***Father T.G. Morrow***

## ROMANTIC LOVE / MARRIAGE

It is biblical to start by examining the plank in your own eye before attempting to help someone remove the sliver from theirs, so the first source of disappointment I discuss will be romantic love. It is my present plank, so to speak, in that I have officially been unmarried for over a decade longer than I imagined. In Bible college my greatest fear was leaving single and becoming a single missionary. At that point in time it seemed like a curse. Now, close to fifteen years later, some days it still seems like a curse. Then there are weeks and months when I am completely fine with it, even thankful for it!

Singleness has some definite perks. Aside from answering to God and my employer, I can pretty much do what I want, when I want. I can stay up and get up as late as desired, leave paperwork spread out all over the living room for as long as necessary, spend money without clearing it with another person, eat out a meal or two a day, and sleep through the night without interruption. I also have the freedom to control the TV remote, to leave the bed unmade or the dishes undone, and to develop close friendships with multiple guys.

Singleness has enabled me to truly identify who I am including my character flaws, weaknesses and patterns of sin, and work on them before involving another person. It has illuminated my strengths and capabilities together with personal accomplishments I never would have dreamed possible.

Immediately following college graduation, I took a ten-day trip to London and Paris with close to fifty students from my graduating class. Soon after returning home from that trip, I began working to pay off college debt and raising support to get to Germany as a missionary. It took me two and a half years to raise what I needed, and in that time I had the opportunity to share my passion for missions in well over 100 churches throughout Pennsylvania, Ohio, New York, Indiana, Illinois, Michigan, Iowa and Alaska, showing me that I have some giftedness as a public speaker. This was news to me, especially after receiving a C in my college speech class.

In April 2004 I said goodbye, left everything and everyone I knew, and moved across the ocean following a container carrying all of my belongings. I settled into an apartment right outside of Berlin in the former East, just yards from where the Berlin wall stood. I have lived alone ever since, ministering to children and teenagers in an international English-speaking church.

With the help of God and by His grace alone, I have learned a second language (albeit imperfectly), led many young people to Christ, housed an average of 150 days of houseguests each year, begun writing three books (of which this is one), and started studying for a Master in Church History. These were all items on my life "bucket list," but I would not have had time to accomplish half of them with a husband and children. God's decision and will for singleness for this time of my life is no longer a mystery.

## THE CHURCH'S RESPONSE

"Godliness with contentment is great gain" (1 Timothy 6:6), but it is rare. To encounter a person who truly desires marriage but is unmarried and choosing contentment is a beautiful thing. Contentment should be viewed as a godly response. Typically, though, this is not the case.

"What is wrong with me? Something must be wrong or I would be married and having children." Unfortunately, this is the way the Christian community makes single, infertile or barren people feel. Something went wrong.

I turned the big "3-0" a few years ago and have definitely been the recipient of comments like, "Don't worry, a friend of mine just got married at 38 and now she's pregnant! There's still time." Or there is the popular, "Have you tried 'eHarmony'?" It is as if marriage is the goal of life, and everything else is a just an appetizer—something to calm your cravings while you wait. This thought that something is wrong if we are not in a relationship or able to bear a child is so common that it must be linked to our culture.

The Christian community probably worries about singleness and childlessness because of the emphasis the Bible puts on marriage and the family. However, we should be concerned that the church is in a state of panic. Just type "Christian Singles" into Google and you will find pages upon pages of Christian on-line dating services. Type "Christian Dating and Courtship" into Amazon.com and discover scores of books voicing varied opinions and advice.

I am single and can say from experience that my believing friends and family are often more concerned about my single state than I am. We want our loved ones to be happy, but unfortunately we think that somehow happiness will magically come as a result of tying the knot and reproducing. What is truly unfortunate is that if a single person miraculously reaches a point of contentment, ignoring the advice and pity of well-meaning brothers and sisters in Christ, people then begin to wonder if the person is gay! What a mess we are making!

The tragedy is that the church reacts to ALL singleness as a problem that needs solving. In fact, singleness can be a gift from God and the *will* of God, even if only for a season. If it is in fact the will of God for a time, then it is to be embraced and lived out for the glory of God. Jim Elliot is quoted saying, "Live to the hilt every situation you believe to be the will of God. Wherever you are, be all there" (E. Elliot, Through Gates of Splendor 20).

## SOCIETY'S RESPONSE

Ironically, the world is much less concerned about this. There are two main reasons for this, the first being that our society has turned its back on absolute truth. Of course marriage is not a big deal! You can just sleep around and have fun where fun is to be found. The second reason is that the world views other goals as equal to, or more important than, marriage and family. A successful, fulfilling career is taking over, at least in America, as a superior goal. This is true in Germany as well.

Examples of this can, of course, be found in the media. The shift happened pretty obviously in the progression of situation comedies. The 1950s introduced us to the first sitcoms: *I Love Lucy, Father Knows Best, Leave it to Beaver* and *The Donna Reed Show*. The 60s followed with: *The Andy Griffith Show, My Three Sons, The Dick Van Dyke Show, The Patty Duke Show,* and *The Brady Bunch*.

The 70s gave us *The Mary Tyler Moore Show, All in the Family, The Bob Newhart Show, The Waltons, Happy Days, Laverne and Shirley, Three's Company, Benson, The Facts of Life,* and *Little House on the Prairie*. The 80s were, of course *Cheers, Family Ties, Silver Spoons, Golden Girls, Growing Pains, The Cosby Show, Who's the Boss?, Married with Children, Roseanne,* and *The Wonder Years*. The shift is already obvious. In just a 10-year time span between the 60s and 70s, we see the breakdown of the American family when shows like *Laverne and Shirley* and *Three's Company* became popular. In these shows, marriage was an option and perhaps still a goal, but the single life was becoming attractive. This was not true in America in the 50s. Possibly it was the independence of the 1960s that sent us spiraling downward.

With *Who's the Boss?, Married with Children* and *Roseanne,* the 80s proposed that all families are dysfunctional and we need to learn to laugh at family life. *The Simpsons, Family Matters,* and *Full House* led us into the 90s, followed by *Step by Step, The Fresh Prince of Bel Air, Seinfeld, Frasier, Home Improvement, Will and Grace,* and last but certainly not least, *Friends,* "the most popular U.S. sitcom of the 1990s-2000s" (sitcom). Most of the 90s shows were still centered on the family institution, but it was quickly becoming more and more dysfunctional. Family values were gone, and never before in history had singleness and selfishness been as celebrated as on shows like *Friends* and *Seinfeld.*

In our new millennium it is hard to find a TV show centered on the family. You may know nothing at all about television, but if you do you will notice how much things are changing. Most of these shows have carried over to Europe. I can turn on my TV in Berlin and find many of the bigger hits listed above, including the older ones. TV is certainly a representation of the decline in the family structure. The cause is a departure from biblical truth. Take God out of a culture and the culture will become godless. It's common sense.

**A GOD-CENTERED RESPONSE**

The desire for a mate is a fine one. It is God-given. After all, who thought of marriage? Or who thought of sex for that matter? God! What a concept: God as the inventor of sex! We don't often think of God that way, but as a friend once reminded me, God is the inventor of everything except for evil. (Evil had a different inventor.)

This desire for a life partner or mate starts off purely enough. We just want what God has put in our hearts, what He has granted most of His creation. After all, the majority of people marry or at least procreate. I do not know the recent statistics worldwide, but a census taken of the United States in 2000 shows that, "Among the 221.1 million people aged 15 and over in the United States:

- 120.2 million, or 54.4 percent, were now married;
- 41.0 million, or 18.5 percent, were widowed, divorced or separated; and
- 59.9 million, or 27.1 percent, were never married" (Kreider).

54.4 percent of Americans age 15 and over were married in the year 2000. Another 18.5 percent had been married previously and

72.9 percent of Americans over age 15 had said marriage vows at some point when this survey was taken. That is an overwhelming majority! This desire isn't ridiculous; it is simply a wish for what almost everybody else finds: a mate.

Here are some verses to ponder as you think through this issue:

*"He who finds a wife finds what is good and receives favor from the Lord" (Proverbs 18:22).*

*"A wife of noble character who can find? She is worth far more than rubies" (Proverbs 31:10).*

*"The Lord God said, 'It is not good for man to be alone. I will make a helper suitable for him'" (Genesis 2:18).*

*"Now for the matters you wrote about: It is good for a man not to marry. But since there is so much immorality, each man should have his own wife, and each woman her own husband" (1 Corinthians 7:1, 2).*

*"Now to the unmarried and the widows I say: It is good for them to stay unmarried, as I am. But if they cannot control themselves, they should marry, for it is better to marry than to burn with passion" (1 Corinthians 7:8, 9).*

*"Nevertheless, each one should retain the place in life that the Lord assigned to him and to which God has called him. This is the rule I lay down in all the churches. Was a man already circumcised when he was called? He should not become uncircumcised. Was a man uncircumcised when he was called? He should not be circumcised. Circumcision is nothing and uncircumcision is nothing. Keeping God's commands is what counts. Each one should remain in the situation which he was in when God called him. Were you a slave when you were called? Don't let it trouble you—although if you can gain your freedom, do so. For he who was a slave when he was called by the Lord is the Lord's freedman; similarly, he who was a free man when he was called is Christ's slave. You were bought at a price; do not become slaves of men. Brothers, each man, as responsible to God, should remain in the situation God called him to" (1 Corinthians 7:17-24).*

*"Now about virgins: I have no command from the Lord, but I give a judgment as one who by the Lord's mercy is trustworthy. Because of the present crisis, I think that it is good for you to remain as you are. Are you married? Do not seek a divorce. Are you unmarried? Do not look for a wife. But if you do marry, you have not sinned; and if a virgin marries, she has not sinned. But those who marry will face many troubles in this life, and I want to spare you this" (1 Corinthians 7:25-28).*

*"I would like you to be free from concern. An unmarried man is concerned about the Lord's affairs—how he can please the Lord. But a married man is concerned about the affairs of this world—how he can please his wife—and his interests are divided. An unmarried woman or virgin is concerned about the Lord's affairs: Her aim is to be devoted to the Lord in both body and spirit. But a married woman is concerned about the affairs of this world—how she can please her husband. I am saying this for your own good, not to restrict you, but that you may livein a right way in undivided devotion to the Lord" (1 Corinthians 7:32-35).*

*"As for younger widows, do not put them on such a list. For when their sensual desires overcome their dedication to Christ, they want to marry. Thus they bring judgment on themselves, because they have broken their first pledge. Besides, they get into the habit of being idle and going about from house to house. And not only do they become idlers, but also gossips and busybodies, saying things they ought not to. So I counsel younger widows to marry, to have children, to manage their homes and to give the enemy no opportunity for slander" (1 Timothy 5:11-14).*

These point out that **it is good to marry, and it is also good to remain unmarried.** The Apostle Paul refers to the ability to remain unmarried and undividedly devoted to God as a "gift" (1 Corinthians 7:7).

Companionship was the need of the first person ever created. "Then the Lord God said, 'It is not good for the man to be alone. I will make a helper as his complement'" (Gen. 2:18, HCSB). In naming the animals, Adam may have realized that for every *he* there was a *she*, except in his case. "But for the man no helper was found as his complement" (2:20). I do not think Adam realized he desired a mate specifically, but God knew what would fulfill him. Our desire for a human "complement" is natural and good; however, we do not usually leave it with God to fulfill. We begin there, but then the clock starts ticking, time moves quickly and patience runs thin. Soon we're 16, then 18, then 20, then—horrors!—out of college, and then the unthinkable: approaching 30! The natural next step is doubt.

**OUR RESPONSE: A CHOICE**

*God doesn't care about your desire.*

Wait, what was that?

*God doesn't care about your desire.*

Well, surely that's not true. What about Psalm 37:4? "Delight yourself in the Lord and He will give you the desires of your heart."

*Yes, but has it happened?.*

Hmmm . . . no . . . actually, it hasn't.

*Haven't you waited patiently for a very long time?*

Ummm . . . actually, yes . . . I have.

*Haven't you prayed about it MANY times?*

Yes! Thousands of times!

*So, if asking God and waiting isn't the answer, then shouldn't you just help yourself a little?*

Hmm . . . that doesn't seem like such a bad idea. I mean, I have heard that God helps those who help themselves. (That is in the Bible, right?) Maybe God's busy with bigger things like managing the universe. Perhaps this little desire of mine for romantic love isn't one of those desires He hurries to fill. But what about all the people in the Bible He did care about: Adam & Eve, Jacob & Rachel, Leah, Ruth, Rahab . . . The list goes on and on. God cares!

*Yeah, but those were the patriarchs. You're nobody.*

Yeah, that's probably true . . .

I could go on and on with this dialogue, but we all know that we begin to doubt God's goodness. "God is holding out on you. He's not really interested in your happiness. You've got to take matters into your own hands, get control of things, arrange for your own happiness" (Eldredge 71). Sound familiar? It is a paraphrase of the serpent's words to Eve from Genesis chapter two. Satan's deception worked then, and he is still using that line of reasoning with us today.

After doubt creeps in, we begin to formulate a plan. The plan is called "How to manipulate God and get Him to respond, or take back the control from Him." Sounds like a complicated plan, but it is quite simple really. When prayer does not work, we try other things to soothe our unfulfilled longings. We might indulge in chocolate, especially if we are female. Men may soothe themselves with a little "eye candy" instead of real candy. Women can do this, too, of course. For instance, how quickly do we turn on those romantic comedies? For some, alcohol is the cure-all; for others, masturbation is a temporary fix.

We know that gluttony, drunkenness and lust are wrong, so we confess these sins to God and try to begin trusting Him again, but now we know that it is possible to temporarily feel better. "Each person is tempted when they are dragged away by their own evil desire and enticed" (James 1:14). *A little won't hurt,* we think. *It'll keep me from bigger sins;* but unless we turn around and RUN back to Christ at this point, the little indulgences will grow. "Then, after desire has conceived, it gives birth to sin; and sin, when it is full-grown, gives birth to death" (James 1:15).

We long for romance and to be loved, but sometimes it does not happen the way we want it to or within our desired timetable, so we are disappointed and disillusioned. Our self-appointment to be happily married by such and such an age did not happen—or perhaps it did, but now marriage is not all we thought it would be. Now we have three options: attempt to manipulate God, take back control of the situation from Him or, of course, the difficult option of trusting Him.

As I write this I am—praise God—turning around and running back to Christ with this very issue. It would be easier to take control, but the truth is that I want Him to have it. If true love ever comes to me, I want it to be from God. How sweet it is when we realize that a gift was God-given! How sweet it must have been for Adam! Believe me, if it is not from God, you do not want it! Ask King David how bitter it is when you take this desire into your own hands.

Here is an important principle to remember: **many times, when we lay our desires on the altar of God's will, they are given back to us more wonderfully and miraculously than we could have ever dreamed.** Personally, I want it to happen that way or no way. My favorite author taught me to live with this desire as my greatest one: "Teach us to desire Your will – nothing more, nothing less, and nothing else" (E. Elliot, Keep A Quiet Heart 126). If that is our desire, we will NEVER be disappointed. It is impossible. Oh, to never experience it again!

How can I be so sure? The same way I know that Jesus loves me: the Bible tells me so. Romans 5:1-5 tells us that "suffering produces perseverance; perseverance, character; and character, hope. And hope does not disappoint us . . ." Hope in what? "We have put our hope in the living God" (1 Timothy 4:10). The Psalmist knew all about disappointment when he penned these words in Psalm 42:5, "Why are you downcast, O my soul? Why so disturbed within me? Put your hope in God, for I will yet praise Him, my Savior and my God." And then again in Psalm 146:5, "Blessed is he . . . whose hope is in the LORD his God." How is someone blessed by hoping in the LORD? If hope in God does not disappoint, then the blessing is the absence of disappointment. If God is your only hope, you will never experience disappointment. Wouldn't *that* be a blessing?!

## NOW WHAT?

This is very personal for me. There are times when I am tempted to go to God in prayer in bitterness of spirit and to accuse Him of not caring, as the disciples did in the midst of the storm in Matthew 8. Every time we focus on the storm instead of the Savior, we will assuredly doubt. Peter did it when he took his eyes off Jesus and focused on the waves. The disciples were rebuked for it right before Jesus rebuked the storm itself.

I had my eyes on the waves and the storm all this week until my brother reminded me of why Peter began to sink. I know the story; I just forget to put it into practice. I need to personalize those waves.

The waves need to be labeled, so that I know precisely on what *not* to put my focus.

Picture in your mind that story of Peter walking on the water. You can see it, can't you? "Then Peter got down out of the boat, walked on the water and came toward Jesus. But when he saw the wind, he was afraid and, beginning to sink, cried out, 'Lord, save me!'" (Matthew 14:29, 30).

If the story stopped there, we might infer that Peter had done nothing wrong. In fact, he succeeded in walking on the water. He took steps on top of a raging sea! That is quite an accomplishment. As far as I know, no one has done it since. However, the next verse cues us in to the fact that Simon Peter did something wrong. Verse 31 says, "Immediately Jesus reached out his hand and caught him. 'You of little faith,' he said, 'why did you doubt?'" This was a rebuke. Peter doubted and began to sink because of doubt.

So, in your mind, label your waves. What are they for you? What or who is it that causes you to doubt God? Do not continue reading until you take as long as is necessary to identify these stumbling blocks, because you can bet that Satan has identified them and knows exactly what he can use to distract us and get us to doubt God's goodness.

Those things need to be off limits. If they can get your eyes off Christ and cause anxiety and bitterness, if they are able to diminish or destroy your joy and peace, then cast them aside! Simon Peter should have stared directly into Christ's face. Oh, if only I could learn from his mistake!

Maybe the desire for romantic love is wreaking havoc in your heart. Should it have that power? If we allow it, the desire for human love and companionship can cause us to doubt God. The desire grows when we shift our focus from God to the desire itself and allow our minds to dwell there for any length of time. We decide where to set up our tent and "camp" mentally.

It is very similar to someone catching a glimpse of a sexually explicit scene on television and making the decision to continue watching that channel instead of shutting it off. The desire morphs into something much more harmful all too quickly because we chose to dwell on it, and every time we feed it, it will grow! The desire for love or marriage or children or sexual satisfaction or just happiness can balloon into an obese fixation if we allow it to become our focus, our aim, our purpose. Before we even realize it is happening, it can develop from a desire into an obsession. A simple wish can become our waking thought each morning and the last conscious consideration at night.

Do you have a desire that brings you to tears when someone else brings it up? That is a good sign that it is becoming more than just a desire. Somewhere deep down inside of you, it is beginning to choke you. Let it grow and it will suffocate you until you cry out, as Peter did, "Lord, save me!"

It does not have to go like that. We can choose to trust and to turn our eyes upon Jesus. "Be anxious for nothing . . ."(Philippians 4:6, NKJV). When is the last time you were anxious for **nothing**? My guess is that you picked up this book because it has been a while. Disappointment has crept in and is growing.

How long have you wandered? Now is the time to begin walking back toward Christ—toward peace. The fact of the matter is, we would give anything for peace. Unfortunately we believe it will come if we can just acquire our desire. And that, my friend, is Satan's greatest lie.

## TRUST GOD'S GOODNESS

Now that you have labeled your wave(s) and identified which desires are tripping you up, keeping you from staring only at Christ, let them go. If it is romantic love you are after, place that desire on the back burner. It should not be your ultimate desire. Let God give it to you if He wants. If your overwhelming desire is for a child, take the advice found in Philippians 4:6, 7. "Do not be anxious about anything, but in everything, by prayer and petition, with thanksgiving, present your requests to God." If you are petitioning God with an anxious heart, you have not yet succeeded. "With thanksgiving, present your requests to God."

Then what? Trust Him. Put off your desire and put on trust! You may say, "How on earth can I do that? It's always on my mind! I will never not desire it." Well, it is like any other desire. If the giant, triple-layer chocolate cake is right in front of me on my kitchen counter and I can see it and smell it, I am not going to be able to focus on much else. If I give it away and it is no longer accessible, the desire for it is not as intense. It's logical.

God knows my desires. I have told Him, and even if I hadn't, He knows my heart, He knows my thoughts, and He knows my words before they are even on my tongue. He knows. Trust Him. If the desire is the best possible thing for you, He will give it to you. If not, He won't. "No good thing does he withhold from those whose walk is blameless" (Psalm 84:11). Praise God!

Here is a little story from John Piper that might help put things into perspective:

> *Many of our prayers will be for things we do not know to be God's will. So we will whisper, "Yet, not my will but thine be done." And we will believe, on the basis of Romans 8:28, that if our specific request is denied, it is because God is preparing something better for us. This fits so well with Matthew 7:9-11. "What man of you, if his son asks of him bread, will give him a stone? Or if he asks for a fish, will give him a serpent? If you, then, who are evil know how to give good gifts to your children, how much more will your Father who is in heaven give good things to those who ask Him?" That is what God will always give in response to our prayers—good things. "No good thing will He withhold from those walk uprightly." If God denies our bread or our fish, it is not to give us a stone or a serpent, but cake and steak.*
>
> *When my one year old, Abraham, sees a shiny kitchen knife and wants to have it, I will divert his attention from it to a big, green can filled with clothespins and show him how much fun they are. Have I answered his prayer? No, I haven't given the specific thing he asked for, but, yes, I did answer his longing to have a good time playing with something.*
>
> *Day before yesterday we opened a box of oatmeal cookies for dessert and they were moldy, so I started to throw them all away. But Benjamin started to cry and say, "I saw one that didn't have fuzz on it." But I said, "Benjamin, the mold starts to grow before you can see it, and it can make you sick. Let's have gorp [good old raisins and peanuts] instead." So we did, but Benjamin felt like he was definitely getting second best. And that's the way we often feel when some of our specific requests are turned down. We think God is giving us second best. But he is not. To those who love him and are called according to his purpose, he always gives what is best for them. Therefore, when we pray, we may always have undoubting faith that God will give us what is best for us (Piper, What Do Answers to Prayer Depend On? Part 2).*

What is it you want more than anything in the world? If your answer is anything other than God and His will, your desires need to be realigned, and that is the purpose of the Word of God. "But seek first his kingdom and his righteousness, and all these things [your needs] will be given to you as well" (Matthew 6:33).

If the Lord is our Shepherd, then we can trust Him. As sheep, we can believe wholeheartedly that the Shepherd will, as Psalm 23 reminds us, give us rest and refreshment, provide clean water and ample grass to feed on, lead us down the right paths, be with us wherever we go, protect us from our enemies, protect us from *ourselves*, heal us, anoint us with His blessing, overflow our cup with His goodness, follow us with His mercy; and if that were not enough, when it is all over, we will dwell in the house of the Lord forever! What more can we ask that He has not already promised? It is time to lay our desires at His feet, trust Him and say, "The Lord is my shepherd, which is all I want." The Lord is my shepherd, I will not be disappointed.

**MARRIAGE**
Discussion Questions

1. Has romantic love been a disappointment in some way in your life, whether as a single or married person? If so, how?

2. How have you dealt with this particular disappointment? Do you find yourself taking it to God and desiring His will, or do you sense yourself holding tightly to *your* will?

3. Why do you think God allows our desire for human love to go unsatisfied at times?

4. If your desire for romantic love is going unmet, do you think it is possible that it is God's will for you at this time? Why or why not?

5. What are the "waves" in your personal storm (see Matthew 14:28-33)? Take a moment to identify the circumstances that are distracting you from fully trusting God or causing you to doubt His goodness.

6. When is the last time you were anxious for **nothing**, completely free of anxiety? If it has been awhile, ask God to help you turn your eyes upon Him and focus on His love for you.

7. What is it you seek more than anything in the world? Look up Matthew 6:33. What *should* be your answer?

# CHAPTER THREE
# FAMILY

*"Let's never forget that some of His greatest mercies are His refusals. He says no in order that He may, in some way we cannot imagine, say yes. All His ways with us are merciful. His meaning is always love."*
**Elisabeth Elliot • Keep a Quiet Heart**

*"But may the righteous be glad and rejoice before God; may they be happy and joyful. Sing to God, sing in praise of his name, extol him who rides on the clouds; rejoice before him—his name is the LORD. A father to the fatherless, a defender of widows, is God in his holy dwelling. God sets the lonely in families . . ."*
**Psalm 68:3-6a**

*"Truly I tell you," Jesus replied, "no one who has left home or brothers or sisters or mother or father or children or fields for me and the gospel will fail to receive a hundred times as much in this present age: homes, brothers, sisters, mothers, children and fields—along with persecutions—and in the age to come eternal life."*
**Mark 10:29-30**

I recently attended the funeral of a 92-year-old man. Included among the mourners were over 90 family members, which is almost one relative per year of his very long life. The legacy he left behind was amazing – and most of them were believers! Surely not many of us will have that many relations in attendance at our funeral, but I think most of us desire what that man had: family.

This is a deep desire, and a source of pain for many. "Data from the 2002 NSFG [National Survey of Family Growth] showed that an estimated 12% of women (7.3 million) in the United States had impaired fecundity or difficulties conceiving or bringing a pregnancy to term" (Chandra, Copen, Stephen).

I definitely desire to be married, but my "biological clock" is not ticking too hard for babies, for which I am thankful. I feel great compassion for my single friends who intensely desire children and feel that time is quickly running out. Several married friends are struggling or have struggled with infertility. Because this is not a pressing issue for me I have asked my friend, Mindy, to allow me to share some of her story with you as it relates to this particular disappointment.

## MINDY STEIN'S STORY

Mindy is an American married to a German pastor. They also live in the capital city of Berlin, and I have had the privilege of forming a friendship with Mindy. Married in their early twenties, Stephan and Mindy did what many couples do and enjoyed married life a few years before deciding to start a family.

It was around that exact same time, at age 26, that a fibroid tumor was discovered on Mindy's uterus. After the fibroid operation Stephan and Mindy were told the crushing, life-altering news that the tumor was cancerous and that her uterus had to be removed. Right before they heard the news though, Mindy "strongly sensed God being almost physically there in the hospital room."

"The decision to have the surgery to remove my uterus was a total roller coaster," Mindy told me. "I was angry, and I kept thinking, *No, this can't be happening!* We prayed for a miracle, but no miracle came. My husband decided that he would rather have me alive so, reluctantly, we decided to go through with it."

I asked Mindy if and how she sensed God's presence and comfort during that time. "Following the surgery," she explained, "my mother flew over to Germany to be with me. Her visit was definitely a comfort. I was also provided a place in a luxurious recovery clinic, and somehow, miraculously, we never had to pay for it; the bill just never showed up."

The trial continued though. "Following the first chemo treatment, I developed an infection. I questioned God, *'Haven't I already been through enough?'* I was losing weight, losing hair and losing faith. This was the hardest point. Despite everything though, after my husband and I spent time crying and grieving, we decided together, before God and our family and friends, not to be bitter."

Mindy told me her story at a local Berlin coffee shop only a year after her battle with cancer. Four surgeries and approximately five months of chemo later, her life has completely changed. She has had to deal with the fact that she and Stephan will never have biological children. That dream is dead. However, Stephan and Mindy continue to serve God side by side as pastor and wife. It would be more than obvious, if you could sit down with Mindy as I did, that she loves the Lord. Mindy was cancer-free by the time she shared her story with me, but the real victory is that Stephan and Mindy are in the process of defeating a more dangerous disease.

Disappointment is truly a subtle path away from Christ. Many people have started out on the journey of following Christ only to end up far away from Him. Disappointment very often transforms into bitterness, and bitterness is an evil weed which, if allowed to grow, will choke out any and all spiritual life. Bitterness is not only an evil weed, it is a tool in the hands of the Evil One himself, a foothold on which the Devil can gain access to the heart. "Keep your heart with all vigilance, for from it flow the springs of life" (Proverbs 4:23, ESV).

We must guard our hearts against bitterness with all vigilance, lest hope in God be choked out. "The thief comes only to steal and kill and destroy," but Christ is the abundant life giver (John 10:10)! Regardless of what the curse destroys, hope and life are restored by returning to Life Himself.

**BIBLICAL EXAMPLES OF MANIPULATION**

Women all through the Bible reached points of despair upon realizing that they were barren, including Sarah, Hannah, Rachel and Leah. This despair drove these women to unfortunate responses.

Sarah convinced her husband to sleep with the maid and have a child through her. Appointing a surrogate mother is one thing, but telling your husband to have sex with another woman is evidence of a woman gone mad! It is very unfortunate that Sarah did not choose to simply wait on God, because although her plan produced an heir, it was not the heir that God had promised to give her in His time.

Hannah went to the temple and "in bitterness of soul" (1 Samuel 1:10, KJV) wept and prayed to God to give her a son, going as far as making a vow to give the child back to God if God would grant her request. Because of her bitterness, this woman ended up giving the child she had waited on for so long over to an old man whose own sons were described as "scoundrels" who "had no regard for the Lord" (1 Samuel 2:12).

Rachel and Leah were sisters married to the same man. Rachel was her husband Jacob's favorite wife, but it was Leah who was able to produce the first three heirs.

> *When Rachel saw that she was not bearing Jacob any children, she became jealous of her sister. So she said to Jacob, "Give me children, or I'll die!" Jacob became angry with her and said, "Am I in the place of God, who has kept you from having children?" Then she said, "Here is Bilhah, my servant. Sleep with her so that she can bear children for me and I too can build a family through her." So she gave him her servant Bilhah as a wife. Jacob slept with her, and she became pregnant and bore him a son. Then Rachel said, "God has vindicated me; he has listened to my plea and given me a son." Because of this she named him Dan. Rachel's servant Bilhah conceived again and bore Jacob a second son. Then Rachel said, "I have had a great struggle with my sister, and I have won." So she named him Naphtali. When Leah saw that she had stopped having children, she took her servant Zilpah and gave her to Jacob as a wife. Leah's servant Zilpah bore Jacob a son. Then Leah said, "What good fortune!" So she named him Gad. Leah's servant Zilpah bore Jacob a second son. Then Leah said, "How happy I am! The women will call me happy." So she named him Asher (Genesis 30:1-12).*

Once again we see a wife (or two wives in this case) telling her husband to sleep with another woman in order to produce an heir. In this case the four women involved – two wives and two maidservants —ended up bearing a total of twelve sons who became heads of the twelve tribes of Israel.

One of the most important things to note in these stories is that all four women could have chosen to trust God and wait on Him, thus avoiding the anxiety, bitterness, unnecessary vows, marital stress and general unhappiness that we see exemplified in these biblical accounts. Hannah is the only one who did not take matters into her own hands, although she did resort to manipulation: "give me what I want and I will . . ."(my paraphrase).

How often are we tempted to make a plea bargain with God to get Him to act in accordance with our desires? How different Hannah's approach was from the approach laid out for us in Philippians chapter four which says, "Do not be anxious about anything, but in everything, by prayer and petition, with thanksgiving, present your requests to God. And the peace of God, which transcends all understanding, will guard your hearts and your minds in Christ Jesus" (v. 6-7). Did Hannah need to manipulate God? I do not think so, and it is pretty clear from the passage that she did not experience the peace of God that comes as a result of presenting requests to Him —not with anxiety, but with thanksgiving.

For what could Hannah have been thankful? She could have thanked God for her loving and understanding husband (see 1 Samuel 1:4-8) who desired her happiness above her fertility. She could have praised God, acknowledging that He alone opens and closes the womb and therefore must have a reason for having kept hers closed for a time. In chapter two of 1 Samuel, after Hannah received what she wanted, she praised God and remarked, "The LORD brings death and makes alive" (v. 6).

A verse from 1 Samuel chapter 3 is posted in my home where it is visible daily. In verse 18, Eli says to young Samuel, "He is the LORD; let Him do what is good in His eyes." Perhaps I am misinterpreting the situation with Hannah, but *my* desire is the "peace of God, which transcends all understanding." Instead of approaching God with a bitter spirit, how much better to have a heart attitude that says, "He is the LORD; let Him do what is good in His eyes." I want to act in accordance with His desires, rather than attempt to manipulate Him to act in accordance with *mine*.

There is another quotation in my home which says, "There are only two kinds of people in the end: those who say to God, 'Thy will be done,' and those to whom God says, in the end, '*Thy* will be done'" (Martindale 293). I want to be in the first category.

## THE WILL OF GOD

How can a person tell if their state in life is the will of God, whether it be singleness or barrenness? God enjoys satisfying our good desires (Psalm 37:4; 103:5; 145:16, 19). Psalm 127:3 tells us that, "Children are a heritage from the LORD, offspring a reward from him." If you have laid your desire before God, and He has not delivered, it is safe to assume that His answer was either "no" or "wait." Since we often do not know which it is, the best thing to do is to wait on Him and live a life that brings Him glory.

"Delight yourself in the Lord and He will give you the desires of your heart" (Psalm 37:4). Focus on delighting in Him – not as a means to an end, but because it should be our greatest privilege and pleasure. When someone or something else, even someone or something good, becomes our "highest joy" or aim, it is idolatry. In Psalm 137:6, for example, the city of Jerusalem is the highest joy, rather than God Himself.

Here is a human illustration that might clarify the biblical principle of waiting for God's will. Recently, I had the task of watching two small children at church while their mothers attended a women's Bible study in an adjacent room. The 3-year-old girl was fine and contentedly watched a video while the almost 2-year-old boy was in a state of panic over realizing his mom had left him. Immediately upon her leaving the room and closing the door behind her, he began to scream and cry. Trying to comfort him, I held him, offered him a snack, and attempted to distract him. He continued to shriek at the top of his lungs for "Mama."

I decided that no amount of screaming or crying was going to move me to go get his mom. She desperately needed to be in the Bible study, and he needed to learn to be without her for an hour. He screamed for several minutes, and began attempting to pull me to the door to open it. He pulled on my fingers for 15 or 20 minutes, screaming the entire time. When I walked around the room in an attempt to distract him with all the fun options, he threw himself at my legs. I was not going to be moved on this issue. He would see his mom soon, but she needed the Bible study. (Thankfully the room was soundproof, and she could not hear this production.)

In the midst of this drama, a truth occurred to me: we do this with God. We tell God that our desire is for such and such (in this case, to go see mommy). When He doesn't immediately respond in the affirmative, we try noise—both volume and quantity. Then praying turns to begging and even crying, and sometimes to a full-blown temper tantrum. Have you ever been there?

Finally, we may try "pulling" God to open the door for us. "God, if You will do this for me, I will . . . give more to the church, become a missionary, etc." If God does not respond in the way or in the time we ask Him to, it is certainly because He has a good reason or a better time!

Have you ever considered that singleness or barrenness might be the will of God for your life—if not forever, at least for a time? To quote the Apostle Paul, "I wish that all men were as I am. But each man has his own gift from God; one has this gift, another has that" (1 Corinthians 7:7). Singleness is a gift from God for as long as it lasts, as is marriage.

To look at it another way, both marriage and children are gifts; they are not rights. In C.S. Lewis' *The Screwtape Letters,* senior devil Screwtape says to junior devil Wormwood: "Whatever men expect, they soon come to think they have a right to; the sense of disappointment can, with very little skill on our part, be turned into a sense of injury" (Martindale 161). We must not ever place our expectations or hope in love, or a person, or a family, for even if we get what we are after, all of these things will disappoint us in time. Placing all your hope in God and in the will of God for your life is the only way to never experience disappointment.

**Here is the truth, plain and simple: if you are not happy now, you will not be happy when you get what you want.** And if you do get what you want, I pity your spouse and children because your happiness is dependent on them! No one can live up to that kind of pressure.

If my hope is in the will of God rather than the hope of romantic love or children, then I am perfectly content either way. If I remain single or barren, my hope rests securely in God, and I am peaceful. If God grants me a spouse or child, then I can accept that gift from Him and rejoice in it for as long as it is given me. If that person is taken from me through death or some other circumstance, my hope will remain in my First Love. I will be content because marriage or having children was never the fulfillment of my hope. (For an incredible example of this kind of trust and contentment, read *Passion and Purity* followed by *Through Gates of Splendor* by Elisabeth Elliot.)

To quote the great Apostle again, "I have learned to be content whatever the circumstances" (Philippians 4:11). This has become the prayer of my heart personally: I desire the will of God—"nothing more, nothing less and nothing else" (E. Elliot, Keep A Quiet Heart 126).

Following the tragic death of his four daughters at sea, Horatio Spafford penned the words to the famous hymn "It is Well with My Soul." Part of the chorus says,

*"Whatever my lot, Thou has taught me to say,*
*It is well, it is well, with my soul."*

Can you say that? Whether you are facing infertility, barrenness, the death of a child, or some other disappointment, ask God today to help you trust Him. I will be the first to admit how shockingly difficult it is to trust God "whatever my lot," but, "As for God, his way is perfect" (Psalm 18:30). We either trust in that, or we don't. Not to trust Him is to say it is NOT well with my soul, which results in great misery. I had to learn that this life is not about me; it's about God. Only after the Spirit began impressing that upon my heart did I grow in trust and begin to experience peace in the midst of heartache and disappointment. My life is about God's will, not the other way around.

**FAMILY**

Discussion Questions

1. Have children or family been a disappointment in some way in your life? If so, how? How have you dealt with this particular disappointment?

2. If your desire for a family or children is going unmet, do you think it is possible that it is God's will for you at this time? Why or why not?

3. How did Mindy Stein's story make you feel about God?

4. Can you honestly say as Eli did in 1 Samuel 3:18, "He is the LORD; let Him do what is good in His eyes."?

5. Can you say that your happiness and hope is in God and His will? If so, are you experiencing peace in the midst of disappointment?

6. Horatio Spafford penned the words to the famous hymn "It is Well with My Soul" after the death of four of his children. "When sorrow like sea billows roll," is it well with your soul? If not, cry out to God today to help you trust Him.

# CHAPTER FOUR
# PEOPLE

*"Let me tell you this: if you meet a loner, no matter what they tell you, it's not because they enjoy solitude. It's because they have tried to blend into the world before, and people continue to disappoint them."*

**Jodi Picoult • My Sister's Keeper**

*"I suppose that since most of our hurts come through relationships so will our healing, and I know that grace rarely makes sense for those looking in from the outside."*

**William P. Young • The Shack**

*"I am like a caravan, lost in the desert while searching for water. Caravans from Tema and Sheba thought they would find water. But they were disappointed, just as I am with you."*

**Job 6:18-20 CEV**

*"To You they cried out and were delivered; in You they trusted and were not disappointed."*

**Psalm 22:5 NASB**

Think back to the last few times you cried. Why did you cry? I cry for a very specific list of reasons. I cry if I am overtired. I cry whenever I hear a sermon or song about lost people needing the Lord. I cry whenever children sing. (Seriously—every single children's Christmas concert—no matter how bad it sounds, and they're not even my kids!) I sometimes cry if a book or movie is really sad or when I feel lonely, but the two main reasons I cry are sin and death. When I cry it is usually a tear or two, not a waterfall; but when somebody I care about makes the choice to live in sin, I'm a mess.

Sin can seem as meaningless as a piece of old gum stuck to the underside of a table. It can also be destructive enough to tear apart an entire family or church. The trick is to never view sin as the piece of old gum: as a small infraction, a careless act, annoying immaturity. If this is our view of sin, it will soon surprise us with its devastation.

I am in full-time ministry so I see sin often, and it is painful every time. Part of my job is to watch for it, to prevent it, so when it happens it is enough to make me angry because I know the consequences. I do get angry; sin makes me angry. The *deceitfulness* of sin makes me angry. I hate that I have lost friends as a result of sin. This just happened to me again recently. A very close friend of mine decided to throw in the towel, spiritually speaking. He walked away from Christ and walked out on our friendship because he loved his sin more. I have cried myself to sleep many nights because of the loss of my friend. I miss him terribly. He left a hole in my life. You cannot just replace friends or buy a new one when the old one breaks.

When I say that people can be a source of disappointment, I mean that it is usually the sin in people that disappoints. Since I am also a sinner, my sin can disappoint me and others. It is important to remember that as much as people disappoint us, we disappoint them!

I am a missionary so, of course, I care deeply about people, but also about things that pertain to missionaries. It is commonly heard in the world of missions, though I can't substantiate it, that the number one reason missionaries leave the field is other missionaries. Before I became a missionary I thought this was ridiculous. Now I know firsthand that it is incredibly true and real.

People disappoint us, plain and simple. I expect my co-workers to be pleased with every single thing I ever do; they're not. I expect them to agree with my opinion on every topic; they don't. However, when I disappoint *them*, I expect them to have limitless patience with me. Of course, life doesn't work that way. As often as my co-workers disappoint me, I have disappointed them. Pride leads us to believe that we—and only we—are RIGHT, and everyone else is wrong!

King David once lamented, "Even my close friend, someone I trusted, one who shared my bread, has turned against me" (Psalm 41:9). "If an enemy were insulting me, I could endure it; if a foe were rising against me, I could hide. But it is you, a man like myself, my companion, my close friend, with whom I once enjoyed sweet fellowship at the house of God, as we walked about among the worshipers" (Psalm 55:12-14). The disciples argued over who was the greatest (Mark 9:33-35). Paul and Barnabas "had such a sharp disagreement that they parted company" (Acts 15:39). Everyone who has ever lived any significant amount of time on this planet has been disappointed by people; it is inevitable.

## CHURCH

Church is one of the greatest sources of disappointment believers and non-believers will face—both the local church and the universal church. My mom repeats this witty little phrase to me sometimes: "CH CH means nothing unless U R in it." Think about it for a moment: it is often the people who *are* in it who make church so hard. People can be so disappointing that they cause us to stop attending church! Even pastors' wives give up on church. It is too difficult or too stressful. People can be just plain mean or live to cause trouble. Unbelievers find church just as disappointing and full of hypocritical, fake "Christians."

I am currently studying to earn a master's degree in church history. The number of arguments, divisions, even religious wars that exist in the pages of the history of the "church" is astounding. The church is a mess. Very rarely do we see the church in the state described in Acts chapter nine: "Then the church throughout Judea, Galilee and Samaria enjoyed a time of peace and was strengthened. Living in the fear of the Lord and encouraged by the Holy Spirit, it increased in numbers" (9:31).

The Bible refers to it as "the church of God, which he bought with his own blood" (Acts 20:28). Christ "loved the church and gave himself up for her to make her holy" (Ephesians 5:25), He feeds and cares for the church (5:29), which is "his body" (Colossians 1:24) and He is "the head" (1:18). When it comes to the church, we must face our disappointments with people and realize it is our APPOINTMENT to care for and build up the church of Christ. Giving up or walking away is not an option. Instead, we must remember that Christ "gave himself up" for the church! It is not about our happiness, satisfaction or pleasure. Following Christ's example, we must give up ourselves for His bride (Revelation 19:7).

Instead of being the delight it should be, church is often a headache and heartache and the hardest place I go all week. I realize in saying this that church is people, not a place, and that is precisely why it is so challenging; but that is also a reflection of my attitude. When I go into the assembly of the believers with my heart and mind focused on giving up myself for Christ and His Church, my perception changes. Attending church becomes the act and place of worship it should be.

## DISAPPOINTMENT GROWS ON TREES

According to biblical history, when did disappointment enter the scene? Disappointment came as a package deal with sin, and with knowledge. The tree from which Eve plucked the fruit was the Tree of the Knowledge of Good and Evil. It grew in the middle of the Garden of Eden next to the Tree of Life. "The LORD God commanded the man. He said, 'You are free to eat from any tree in the garden; but you must not eat from the tree of the knowledge of good and evil, for when you eat from it you will certainly die'" (Genesis 2:16-17).

You have heard it said that "ignorance is bliss." In the Garden of Eden, it was certainly true! The fruit of the knowledge of good and evil literally tasted like disappointment. It was the stereotypical "poisoned apple" of our fairy tales, "good for food and pleasing to the eye, and also desirable for gaining wisdom" (Gen. 3:6) but resulting in death!

I was recently on the island of Madeira, Portugal, for a conference for Western European missionaries. It was my very first taste of the tropics. Dates, mangos and bananas grew everywhere. The beauty of the fruit sold at the markets was unlike any I had laid eyes on in North America or Western Europe. I tried mango, papaya, passion fruit, custard apples and pomegranates, and they were superior to any fruit I had tasted previously. It was "good for food" and "pleasing to the eye," and in no way disappointing.

But the fruit of the tree of knowledge of good and evil led to immediate disappointment with the first bite! Suddenly Eve was a disappointment to Adam as she tempted him to disobey God, and Adam was a disappointment to Eve as he failed to provide spiritual protection and shifted blame onto her. They were disappointed by knowledge as they realized they were naked and felt shame, an unknown sensation up to that point. Then they were disappointed by consequences of "the curse:" loss of paradise, physical pain and suffering, animosity and hostility within once-perfect relationships, separation from God, hard manual labor, sickness and ultimately death. No longer was the fruit of the tree of life available to them, because it would restore their immortality.

In Genesis 4 verse 5, we actually see the first use of the English word *disappointed.* "So Cain became very angry and was disappointed" (GW). His anger and disappointment was with God, which was ironic since it should have been with himself. The Lord confronts Cain with that very fact: "Then the LORD said to Cain, 'Why are you angry? Why is your face downcast? If you do what is right, will you not be accepted? But if you do not do what is right, sin is crouching at your door; it desires to have you, but you must rule over it'" (Genesis 4:6-7). Adam and Eve then must deal with the extreme disappointment of their offspring murdering his brother. Most of us have not had to face a disappointment quite that severe!

Where there are people there is disappointment, which is why Jeremiah pointed out, "Cursed is the one who trusts in man" (17:5). We must love people and serve people, but our hope and trust must be in the only Person who cannot disappoint.

I am not married and therefore have never been disappointed with my spouse or been a disappointment *to* my spouse. I am a little afraid of that potential, but I believe love is worth it should God grant me marriage. Disappointment does not have to kill love. I still love my grandparents, my parents, my siblings, my co-workers . . . the closer the relationship, the greater the chance of disappointment. Marriage is the closest of all the human relationships as it is the only one God has described as merging two into "one flesh" (Gen. 2:24). Commitment, then, has to be the key, along with hope in God.

Recently a friend of mine plummeted into emotional devastation when she discovered her husband was having an affair. Can a marriage recover from that type of disappointment? Obviously there is no easy answer, but what does the Bible have to say?

*"Love your neighbor as yourself" (Jesus, speaking in Mark 12:31).*

Do you truly want to love someone despite crushing disappointments? Start by loving them like you love yourself. Most of us have plenty of grace for our own personal disappointments and sins. Failure to love someone because they have wronged you is wrong. God's love enables us to love even our enemies, and thereby sets us free!

*"But I couldn't even love myself after doing something like that,"* you think.

Then love that person as Christ loves *you*!

*"Walk in the way of love, just as Christ loved us and gave himself up for us as a fragrant offering and sacrifice to God"* (Ephesians 5:2).

I would say the answer is yes, a marriage can recover following infidelity. I have seen it happen. I believe God gives us an ability to love supernaturally. In our own strength it is impossible, but in God's strength all things are possible! We cannot, but in God's strength we can. Jesus looked at them and said, "With man this is impossible, but not with God; all things are possible with God" (Mark 10:27).

## GIVE PEOPLE TO GOD

But what we do with this disappointment? I am not going to go into a discourse on conflict management or peacemaking because there are wonderful resources available on those topics. I *will* say that we should do with this disappointment what we do with other disappointments: give it to God. When I am angry or hurt or frustrated by people, I try to take that wound, that burden, straight to my Heavenly Father, the Shepherd of my soul. Taking it to another person is dangerous because it can result in slander, gossip, or a breaking of confidence. Talking to God about it removes the opportunity for sin, allows us to release it, and produces peace. Remember, God answers prayer!

Many a situation with people has improved because of prayer. God delights in making straight our crooked paths, restoring our relationships and healing our hurts. Again, Psalm 23 tells us he quiets our soul and leads us in paths of righteousness.

I have been tempted more than once to give up as a missionary because of people—amazingly ironic since people are my mission—but it has been over ten years already, and God's Word has always provided the way out of that temptation. "No temptation has overtaken you except what is common to mankind. And God is faithful; he will not let you be tempted beyond what you can bear. But when you are tempted, he will also provide a way out so that you can endure it" (1 Corinthians 10:13).

I have faced some pretty tough disappointments with people. One of the biggest involved the dissolution of my first mission agency due to financial mismanagement. I cannot express how much this hurt, and how many missionaries suffered. In the end, I believe God took care of every individual missionary unit in very unique and special ways, financially and otherwise. My special gift from God to get me through that difficult time involved Him making one of my dreams a reality! This dream was one of those once-in-a-lifetime, pinch yourself, bucket list kind of dreams.

As I mentioned before, immediately following my graduation from Bible college, fifty students from my graduating class took a senior trip to London and Paris. That alone was a dream come true. While on that trip, a few close friends and I took a day trip from London to Oxford. It was love at first sight, and I became absolutely, completely infatuated with the city and its breathtaking spires, colleges, pubs, and bookstores. Oxford is heaven on earth to fans of Oscar Wilde, C.S. Lewis, JRR Tolkien, Lewis Carroll, and Harry Potter. Jump ahead eleven years . . . A few months before the agency I had been a part for ten years dissolved, I saw an advertisement on my church bulletin board in Berlin for Theology Summer School at Oxford University. I snatched the ad, showed it to my pastor, and asked if he would give me some time off to attend some classes. His response was, "Go for it!" So I applied. I have always been academically average, and yet I was accepted into the program. I attended Oxford University and stayed in a private dorm room at Christ Church! The experience was unforgettable.

I studied theology alongside fellow clergy. I ate lunch at The Eagle and Child where Lewis and Tolkien used to meet and discuss their literary masterpieces. All of my dinners were eaten in The Great Hall of Christ Church (aka Hogwarts Hall). One day I took a three and a half hour C.S. Lewis walking tour, explored Magdalen College, walked Addison's Walk, and stood right outside the dorm room where C.S. Lewis knelt and converted to Theism.

People and circumstances disappoint us, but God is the great Dream Giver! He truly is "our refuge and strength, an ever-present help in trouble" (Psalm 46:1). He was with me in my disappointment, helping me see that it was, instead, a new appointment from Him. Maria's line in *The Sound of Music* is true: "When the Lord closes a door, somewhere He opens a window" (Wise). And what a view it was from the window!

**PEOPLE**

Discussion Questions

1. Think back to the last few times you cried. Why was it?

2. When was the last time you were disappointed with someone? What caused the disappointment?

3. When was the last time someone was disappointed with you? How do you wish the person had responded (if they responded less than ideally)?

4. What should you do when you're disappointed with someone? What should you not do? Back up your answer with Scripture.

5. Is church a difficult place for you to go because of people? (Church is the assembly of believers, not a building or location.) What, if anything, can be done to change your heart attitude regarding church or the body of Christ? Again, use Scripture in your answer.

6. Why do you think God allows people to disappoint us?

# CHAPTER FIVE
# SICKNESS

*"In their disappointment, [humans] either become softened toward [God] or they become bolder in their independence. . . . The real underlying flaw in your life is that you don't think that I am good. If you knew I was good and that everything - the means, the ends, and all the processes of individual lives - is all covered by my goodness, then while you might not always understand what I am doing, you would trust me. But you don't. . . . Trust is the fruit of a relationship in which you know you are loved."*
**William P. Young • The Shack**

*"Hope deferred makes the heart sick,
but a longing fulfilled is a tree of life."*
**Proverbs 13:12**

Sickness – physical, emotional, mental, spiritual – touches all of us, and God cares deeply! I was around seven years old when I began getting migraine headaches. I will never forget my first one. I was helping my mom in the church nursery and suddenly the pain, which must have come on progressively, became so bad that I started crying. Crying made my head pound even harder, and I became irrational. A wise, older woman in the nursery with us handed me a small ball and told me to place it under my foot and rub my foot back and forth over it. I have no idea if this actually helped reduce the pain of the headache, but it succeeded in calming me.

My headaches continued for close to 25 years, growing in intensity and frequency. At age 18 I had an MRI to try and identify the problem. No definitive problem was found, and I was told that I likely had arthritis in my neck. Physical therapy helped at the time, but after moving to Germany, the stress of ministry escalated the headaches to a point where I was having trouble coping. By age 31 I was getting four or five bad headaches or migraines a week, and often found myself unconsciously using my fingers to apply pressure above my left eye to stop the pulse that was almost always present. I was suffering and taking what seemed like constant pain medicine, including a prescription for migraines.

One summer, I flew back to the States to speak at a week of junior girls' camp in Iowa. That week I spoke nine times in five days to over 330 campers, and the headaches were so intense that the pain was present almost around the clock. At the end of the week, a bronchial infection landed me in a walk-in medical clinic. The first thing the nurse did was check my blood pressure, which was high enough that I began taking blood pressure medicine immediately.

A couple days later I noticed that I had not had a headache since beginning the medication. Then a week went by without headaches, and then a month, and then six months. It has been over five years, and I have not had a bad headache or migraine since!

I can relate a little bit to this woman's story in Luke chapter eight: "As Jesus was on his way, the crowds almost crushed him. And a woman was there who had been subject to bleeding for twelve years, but no one could heal her. She came up behind him and touched the edge of his cloak, and immediately her bleeding stopped" (Luke 8:43-45). If only every story went like that one, but not all do.

Cancer is a solitary word that contains insurmountable fear and dread . . . and disappointment. We live our lives afraid of it, baffled by it, in search of ways to prevent and avoid it, and praying for protection from the all-too-common threat. Why? Because cancer can kill, and even when it does not, it often means pain and suffering, biopsies, chemo, radiation, hair loss, hospital stays; the list goes on and on. Cancer is not the only sickness we fear, but it is one of the biggest in our lifetime.

Sickness is a BIG disappointment because health is one of our greatest expectations. We hope and expect to live healthy, long lives. We expect this especially for our children, and when this particular "self-appointment" turns into a "dis-appointment" we truly see where our hope was resting because it tears us apart. The sonogram shows deformity; a baby is born with Down syndrome; a child is diagnosed with Cystic Fibrosis; the test comes back positive; the tumor is malignant; the mammogram reveals a lump: disappointment.

God did not promise us lives free of pain, health problems or suffering, and yet we expect it. When we experience any of these things we are surprised, frustrated, even angry and almost certainly disappointed.

> *Therefore we do not lose heart. Though outwardly we are wasting away, yet inwardly we are being renewed day by day. For our light and momentary troubles are achieving for us an eternal glory that far outweighs them all. So we fix our eyes not on what is seen, but on what is unseen, since what is seen is temporary, but what is unseen is eternal (2 Corinthians 4:16).*

To me, this passage promises sickness. Outwardly we are wasting away. It's a fact. There will be physical pain, discomfort and suffering. The loss of health can be a crushing disappointment, whether it happens to us or to someone we love. It has the potential to cause us to doubt God's goodness or power, which is a path that can lead us away from Him. It can also drive us to Him! If we can remember that sickness and physical suffering is God-allowed and even appointed, we can see it as a special assignment, a chance to bring God glory, even a chance to share Christ with someone else suffering in a similar manner.

When I was a little girl around the age of five, my dad was a youth pastor. One of the teenage girls in his youth group was a physical dwarf. This young lady was asked to be a keynote speaker at a convention for the Little People of America. She had the opportunity at the convention to share her faith in Christ. My dad, who is six foot six inches tall, would never have been asked to speak at a Little People's convention, but a teenage girl, because of a particular physical "appointment," had the opportunity to bring God glory in a BIG way!

God allows sickness, handicaps, disabilities, disease, and other physical hardships often because they are unique platforms for His glory. Three of my cousin's four children have cystic fibrosis. Their challenges are drastically different than the challenges of people without CF, but so are their opportunities. The kids and their parents will touch lives of people I cannot, and they will share Christ! God has appointed them to change the world in a way only He can imagine. He is good and we can trust Him no matter how difficult the journey.

For 25 years I suffered with headaches, until five years ago when I was healed by God and blood pressure medication. Compared to many people, I have not truly faced this particular disappointment, for which I am grateful. I have friends who face difficult illness, though. A girlfriend agreed to write out her story so that you might benefit from reading about her experience with the disappointment of loss of health.

## MELODY FRANCIS KING'S STORY

"I have never really considered myself a writer, just someone who has figured out how to get by in that particular department. I honestly believe that God has wanted me to write these words for a while. I don't think I have been avoiding it, just waiting for the proverbial 'perfect' words and timing, as if there are such things. There has definitely been a lot of fear involved in the process as well. It's hard to be real. It makes us vulnerable, and we feel open to attack when we're honest. The bottom line is that honesty and realness are hard and sometimes even painful. They are also healing and cathartic.

I have written some pretty honest posts on Facebook before, until one day when I was feeling particularly vulnerable, I deleted all of them. Truth be told, I've learned that my sharing openly and honestly really isn't about me, although I do reap some wonderful benefits.

Over the course of the past four years, God has and still is helping me understand that my reputation rests securely in His hands. What can man do to me? He has also helped me realize that silence is often a tool wielded destructively by the devil himself. To keep silent about my journey over the past few years is to risk leaving someone else who has perhaps struggled as I have still feeling isolated and alone, perhaps still believing Satan's age-old lie that they are the only one who struggles this way and that they better keep quiet about it, lest someone think ill of them. I can be silent no longer.

In July of 2007, I started experiencing severe insomnia. About a month later, I moved to West Virginia to teach first grade at a wonderful Christian school there. I had a lovely little apartment, I knew a few people from the area from college, and even found a great church. I was a 24-year-old Bible college graduate who finally felt like all her "ducks were in a row." However, the insomnia intensified to the point that I really started to feel like I was losing it. After a week without sleeping, I had an emotional breakdown that landed me in the hospital.

I moved back home with my parents to recover. At the time, I honestly thought I had just had a bad couple of months and figured that I'd be able to get back on my feet within six months. In some ways, I did. A distinct cycle began to manifest itself however, and it was concerning to me as well as my family.

Each month, I would experience a week of severe depression, followed by a week of extremely high energy and insomnia. Then I would be 'normal' for the other two weeks of the month. I saw a psychiatrist regularly and it didn't take him long to diagnose me with Bipolar Disorder.

He started me on an anti-depressant which did nothing for my symptoms, but provided me with a plethora of unpleasant side-effects. During this time I was working with autistic children, work I loved but which was highly stressful. Eventually, the cycle got so intense that I had to give up my job.

My psychiatrist switched me over to another anti-depressant, combined with another new medication that was supposed to be good for people with Bipolar Disorder. It didn't help me and, once again, I was provided with a lovely dose of side-effects.

Finally I decided to go to my regular doctor for a full physical, blood work, etc. to get a second opinion. He looked me straight in the eye and said that I didn't have Bipolar Disorder. He then informed me that my difficulties were purely hormonal and could be easily rectified with birth control pills.

While it did help a little bit, I still experienced the erratic monthly cycle of depression, mania, and then normalcy. I had to give up working once again. Finally I scheduled an appointment with a psychologist (counselor) in the area. After nine weeks, he said he really did think I was suffering from Bipolar Disorder and referred me to a psychiatrist who could make the official diagnosis and begin treatment.

In October of 2010, I made my first visit to a new doctor's office. After meeting with him, he decided to put me on a mood stabilizer. Since that time, my bouts of depression or mania have been much less intense and much easier to manage. As my husband so aptly put it, 'we are cautiously optimistic at this point.' I haven't felt this "normal" in over three years. To be quite honest, I am not exactly sure what to do with the new normal.

I would be remiss if I did not mention two key components in my journey toward wholeness. My heavenly Father has literally not only been with me, but has held me every step of the way (John 10:27, 28). Even in my darkest hour, lying in an emergency room hospital bed, when I cried out to Him, He met me in a very real way. His mercy and faithfulness have become tangibly real to me over the past four years.

When He said He would never leave us or forsake us as His children, He wasn't messing around. I can honestly say that I am thankful for the past few years because I would not know how very kind and personal our God really is had I not walked this path. We do indeed serve an all-powerful, all-knowing, all-wise God! I long for heaven and home where I can be in His presence and worship Him forever and always!

The last thing I want to mention is that through reading and doing a little research, I have found some things that I can do naturally that really help me manage my bipolar disorder on a daily basis, the first being to enjoy sunshine and outdoor exercise. I make it my goal to get outside and take a long, brisk walk every day, even if the sun isn't shining and it's really cold. Exercise and vitamin D are vitally important to every human being, but especially important to anyone who struggles with depression. The other things I have found to be helpful are: 1) making sure I am eating enough dark green, high-iron vegetables every day (I also take an iron supplement), 2) maintaining a similar routine day to day, 3) trying to drink the same amount of caffeine each day, and 4) drinking plenty of water.

Having shared all of this, my hope and prayer is that my story has somehow, in some way, been an encouragement and blessing to you. God, in His infinite mercy, has been more than kind to me, and I am forever grateful! I have experienced some of the darkest days of my life over the past few years and God has shown His loving-kindness, compassion, faithfulness, and mercy over and over and over again. He met me in my darkest hours. His mercies truly are new every morning, His compassion never, ever fails, His grace is sufficient, and His power truly is perfected in our weakness. I would never have come to know how personally kind, loving, and faithful my Savior is had I not walked this road."

**WHY AM I STILL SICK?**

What if God does not heal? What if we pray a thousand times, and He does not answer the way we asked? Many have attempted to deal with these questions. The Word of God offers answers for why God does not always heal. Here are three that I have found:

1. **God wants His grace to be enough.**

   *Therefore, in order to keep me from becoming conceited, I was given a thorn in my flesh, a messenger of Satan, to torment me. Three times I pleaded with the Lord to take it away from me. But he said to me, "My grace is sufficient for you, for my power is made perfect in weakness." Therefore I will boast all the more gladly about my weaknesses, so that Christ's power may rest on me. That is why, for Christ's sake, I delight in weaknesses, in insults, in hardships, in persecutions, in difficulties. For when I am weak, then I am strong (2 Corinthians 12:7b-10).*

2. **God wants to do <u>more</u> than we ask or expect!**

   *Now Jesus loved Martha and her sister and Lazarus. So when he heard that Lazarus was sick, he stayed where he was two more days . . . then he told them plainly, "Lazarus is dead, and for your sake I am glad I was not there, so that you may believe." . . . Jesus, once more deeply moved, came to the tomb. It was a cave with a stone laid across the entrance. "Take away the stone," he said. "But, Lord," said Martha, the sister of the dead man, "by this time there is a bad odor, for he has been there four days." Then Jesus said, "Did I not tell you that if you believe, you will see the glory of God?" So they took away the stone. Then Jesus looked up and said, "Father, I thank you that you have heard me. I knew that you always hear me, but I said this for the benefit of the people standing here, that they may believe that you sent me." When he had said this, Jesus called in a loud voice, "Lazarus, come out!" The dead man came out, his hands and feet wrapped with strips of linen, and a cloth around his face. Jesus said to them, "Take off the grave clothes and let him go" (John 11:5-44).*

We may ask for healing, and God may want to do something greater, something of which our minds cannot yet even conceive. This may include the salvation of souls. It will most definitely include His glory!

3. **God is sovereign and wants us, more than anything, to trust Him!**

Why does God allow physical pain and suffering? The answer is simple. Sickness entered the world when sin did (Romans 5:12). The fall of man in Genesis 3 brought with it a curse that includes physical death or mortality. This means, logically, that sickness will occur, and that not all sickness will be healed. God is sovereign in the choices He makes. Someday, "there will be no more death or mourning or crying or pain, for the old order of things has passed away" (Revelation 21:4). Until then, we must trust His will!

*Oh, the depth of the riches of the wisdom and knowledge of God!*
*How unsearchable his judgments,*
*and his paths beyond tracing out!*
*"Who has known the mind of the Lord?*
*Or who has been his counselor?"*
*"Who has ever given to God,*
*that God should repay them?"*
*For from him and through him and for him are all things.*
*To him be the glory forever! Amen.*
Romans 11:33-36

**SICKNESS**

Discussion Questions

1. Have you ever been disappointed with the loss of health, either your own or the health of someone you love?

2. Do you expect yourself and your loved ones to live long, healthy lives?

3. Has this desire or expectation ever disappointed you? If so, how did you respond?

4. Why does God allow physical pain and suffering? (Feel free to come up with your own answers or refer to the answers offered in the book.)

5. Who is someone who has challenged and/or inspired you spiritually in the way he or she dealt with a loss of health?

6. What are some life lessons one could learn in the midst of sickness that perhaps could not be learned any other way? What are some lessons you have learned in times of sickness (like Melody Francis King)?

7. How do you think a loss of health may be God's appointment instead of a disappointment?

# CHAPTER SIX
# DEATH

*Therefore, just as sin entered the world through one man, and death through sin, and in this way death came to all men, because all sinned."*
**Romans 5:12**

*"There is a connection between heaven and earth. Finding that connection makes everything meaningful, including death. Missing it makes everything meaningless, including life."*
**The Other Side of Heaven • Disney movie 2001**

There are a few stories in the Bible that make me cringe to read them. They are so full of the emotions that accompany disappointment that often, when I read these accounts, I cry along with the characters. I feel their pain and empathize with them. I am going to discuss three such biblical stories, but there are many, many more. Here is a hint: the following three stories all deal with death, life's greatest disappointment.

***THE SHUNAMMITE'S SON RESTORED TO LIFE***
***2 Kings 4:8-37***

*One day Elisha went to Shunem. And a well-to-do woman was there, who urged him to stay for a meal. So whenever he came by, he stopped there to eat. She said to her husband, "I know that this man who often comes our way is a holy man of God. Let's make a small room on the roof and put in it a bed and a table, a chair and a lamp for him. Then he can stay there whenever he comes to us."*

*One day when Elisha came, he went up to his room and lay down there. He said to his servant Gehazi, "Call the Shunammite." So he called her, and she stood before him. Elisha said to him, "Tell her, 'You have gone to all this trouble for us. Now what can be done for you? Can we speak on your behalf to the king or the commander of the army?'"*

*She replied, "I have a home among my own people."*

*"What can be done for her?" Elisha asked.*

*Gehazi said, "Well, she has no son and her husband is old."*

*Then Elisha said, "Call her." So he called her, and she stood in the doorway. "About this time next year," Elisha said, "you will hold a son in your arms."*

*"No, my lord," she objected. "Don't mislead your servant, O man of God!"*

*But the woman became pregnant, and the next year about that same time she gave birth to a son, just as Elisha had told her.*

*The child grew, and one day he went out to his father, who was with the reapers. "My head! My head!" he said to his father. His father told a servant, "Carry him to his mother." After the servant had lifted him up and carried him to his mother, the boy sat on her lap until noon, and then he died. She went up and laid him on the bed of the man of God, then shut the door and went out.*

*She called her husband and said, "Please send me one of the servants and a donkey so I can go to the man of God quickly and return."*

*"Why go to him today?" he asked. "It's not the New Moon or the Sabbath."*

*"It's all right," she said.*

*She saddled the donkey and said to her servant, "Lead on; don't slow down for me unless I tell you." So she set out and came to the man of God at Mount Carmel. When he saw her in the distance, the man of God said to his servant Gehazi, "Look! There's the Shunammite! Run to meet her and ask her, 'Are you all right? Is your husband all right? Is your child all right?' "*

*"Everything is all right," she said.*

*When she reached the man of God at the mountain, she took hold of his feet. Gehazi came over to push her away, but the man of God said, "Leave her alone! She is in bitter distress, but the LORD has hidden it from me and has not told me why."*

*"Did I ask you for a son, my lord?" she said. "Didn't I tell you, 'Don't raise my hopes'?"*

*Elisha said to Gehazi, "Tuck your cloak into your belt, take my staff in your hand and run. If you meet anyone, do not greet him, and if anyone greets you, do not answer. Lay my staff on the boy's face."*

*But the child's mother said, "As surely as the LORD lives and as you live, I will not leave you." So he got up and followed her.*

*Gehazi went on ahead and laid the staff on the boy's face, but there was no sound or response. So Gehazi went back to meet Elisha and told him, "The boy has not awakened."*

*When Elisha reached the house, there was the boy lying dead on his couch. He went in, shut the door on the two of them and prayed to the LORD. Then he got on the bed and lay upon the boy, mouth to mouth, eyes to eyes, hands to hands. As he stretched himself out upon him, the boy's body grew warm. Elisha turned away and walked back and forth in the room and then got on the bed and stretched out upon him once more. The boy sneezed seven times and opened his eyes.*

*Elisha summoned Gehazi and said, "Call the Shunammite." And he did. When she came, he said, "Take your son." She came in, fell at his feet and bowed to the ground. Then she took her son and went out.*

This is such an emotional story! The first thing that struck me when I read this account was the Shunammite woman's response to Elisha when he told her that in a year's time, she would hold a son in her arms. "No, my lord!" she objected. "Please, man of God, don't mislead your servant!"

I am trying to imagine a man of God coming to me and telling me that my greatest heart's desire will be realized by next year. I think I would respond in a similar way. "Please don't get my hopes up! What if what you say doesn't happen? My hopes will be dashed! The disappointment will be too great to bear!"

The woman did become pregnant. Then, only a few years later the son that she had waited so long for died in her arms. She echoes her original objection: *did I ask you for a son? No, I didn't. This was your idea. I told you not to raise my hopes, not to disappoint me and this is what happens? I was better off before! Now, instead of an unfulfilled desire, I have my heart torn out of my chest!!*

Don't you feel for her? The emotion leaps off the page. The Bible is full of these incredibly dramatic, true-life biographical snapshots. This is not a story of the woman's entire life—it is the story of her greatest disappointment, and what God did for her. The resolution is truly bizarre. The Prophet Elisha's servant, Gehazi, obeys Elisha and lays his staff on the dead boy's face. Nothing happens. Then Elisha shows up, prays, lies on the boy two times, the boy sneezes seven times, opens his eyes and his life is restored! What a story!

Another even more gripping story of human disappointment is found in John chapter eleven. This is one of my favorite stories in the whole Bible.

### *THE DEATH OF LAZARUS*
### *John 11:1-44*

*Now a man named Lazarus was sick. He was from Bethany, the village of Mary and her sister Martha. This Mary, whose brother*

*Lazarus now lay sick, was the same one who poured perfume on the Lord and wiped his feet with her hair. So the sisters sent word to Jesus, "Lord, the one you love is sick."*

*When he heard this, Jesus said, "This sickness will not end in death. No, it is for God's glory so that God's Son may be glorified through it." Jesus loved Martha and her sister and Lazarus. Yet when he heard that Lazarus was sick, he stayed where he was two more days.*

*Then he said to his disciples, "Let us go back to Judea."*

*"But Rabbi," they said, "a short while ago the Jews tried to stone you, and yet you are going back there?"*

*Jesus answered, "Are there not twelve hours of daylight? A man who walks by day will not stumble, for he sees by this world's light. It is when he walks by night that he stumbles, for he has no light."*

*After he had said this, he went on to tell them, "Our friend Lazarus has fallen asleep; but I am going there to wake him up."*

*His disciples replied, "Lord, if he sleeps, he will get better." Jesus had been speaking of his death, but his disciples thought he meant natural sleep.*

*So then he told them plainly, "Lazarus is dead, and for your sake I am glad I was not there, so that you may believe. But let us go to him."*

*Then Thomas (called Didymus) said to the rest of the disciples, "Let us also go, that we may die with him."*

*On his arrival, Jesus found that Lazarus had already been in the tomb for four days. Bethany was less than two miles from Jerusalem, and many Jews had come to Martha and Mary to comfort them in the loss of their brother. When Martha heard that Jesus was coming, she went out to meet him, but Mary stayed at home.*

*"Lord," Martha said to Jesus, "if you had been here, my brother would not have died. But I know that even now God will give you whatever you ask."*

*Jesus said to her, "Your brother will rise again."*

*Martha answered, "I know he will rise again in the resurrection at the last day."*

*Jesus said to her, "I am the resurrection and the life. He who believes in me will live, even though he dies; and whoever lives and believes in me will never die. Do you believe this?"*

*"Yes, Lord," she told him, "I believe that you are the Christ, the Son of God, who was to come into the world."*

*And after she had said this, she went back and called her sister Mary aside. "The Teacher is here," she said, "and is asking for you." When Mary heard this, she got up quickly and went to him. Now Jesus had not yet entered the village, but was still at the place where Martha had met him. When the Jews who had been with Mary in the house, comforting her, noticed how quickly she got up and went out, they followed her, supposing she was going to the tomb to mourn there.*

*When Mary reached the place where Jesus was and saw him, she fell at his feet and said, "Lord, if you had been here, my brother would not have died."*

*When Jesus saw her weeping, and the Jews who had come along with her also weeping, he was deeply moved in spirit and troubled. "Where have you laid him?" he asked.*

*"Come and see, Lord," they replied.*

*Jesus wept.*

*Then the Jews said, "See how he loved him!"*

*But some of them said, "Could not he who opened the eyes of the blind man have kept this man from dying?"*

*Jesus, once more deeply moved, came to the tomb. It was a cave with a stone laid across the entrance. "Take away the stone," he said.*

*"But, Lord," said Martha, the sister of the dead man, "by this time there is a bad odor, for he has been there four days."*

*Then Jesus said, "Did I not tell you that if you believed, you would see the glory of God?"*

*So they took away the stone. Then Jesus looked up and said, "Father, I thank you that you have heard me. I knew that you always hear me, but I said this for the benefit of the people standing here, that they may believe that you sent me."*

*When he had said this, Jesus called in a loud voice, "Lazarus, come out!" The dead man came out, his hands and feet wrapped with strips of linen, and a cloth around his face.*

*Jesus said to them, "Take off the grave clothes and let him go."*

Lazarus, Jesus' good friend, is sick. His sisters send word to Jesus because they know that Jesus can make him well, but what does Jesus do instead? He waits. He waits long enough that Lazarus dies.

Unlike the story of the Shunammite woman, this is probably a familiar story to you, especially if you grew up going to Sunday School like I did. I can picture the flannelgraph figures: Mary and Martha in their colorful robes and head coverings, Jesus dressed all in white appearing very busy, and Lazarus lying on a cot with a white sheet covering him. Flannelgraph, though, cannot possibly convey what this must have felt like for Lazarus' sisters. They asked Jesus for help in a time of desperation, fully knowing that he could help!

I have two younger brothers. If one of them was sick and dying, I would do the exact same thing that Mary and Martha did. I would ask everyone I knew to get on their knees and cry out to the Great Physician. If my brother died anyway, it would be heart-breaking. My heart would respond the same way theirs did. "If You had been here, my brother would not have died! Why didn't You do anything? You could have healed him!"

Take it a step further. Picture the after-death scene, the preparation of the body for burial, the grave-side (or tomb-side in this case) ceremony. All the while, they are grieving and wondering why their friend, Jesus, didn't care enough to come and help. Forget help; he didn't even come to the funeral! He did not care. It seems that simple. If you care, you come. Our human, finite minds cannot see it any other way. Their tears were more than just sadness over the passing of their beloved brother. They were mingled with tears of betrayal from a beloved friend, a friend they had trusted, their Lord and God! It was a double loss: the death of a family member and the death of their trust.

Have you ever felt that way about God? You pray and trust Him, and He does the opposite of what you asked Him to do. It hurts because we do not understand how a loving God can ignore our pleas and our tears. We conclude that He doesn't care. We were duped.

I imagine that Mary and Martha must have been thinking and feeling that way. Disappointment with God is harder to bear than disappointment with anyone else. He is perfect. His love is perfect. If the loss of a loved one is painful, then should not God in His love protect us from it?

But He didn't. He waited, He tarried, and He did it on purpose! What could be the loving purpose in waiting? This is exactly why Proverbs 3:5 tells us to "lean not on your own understanding." Our understanding is limited.

I love the times when I am paying close enough attention to life's little details to actually get out of them what God is trying so hard to show me. A few years ago my German friend, Daniela, and her 1-year-old son, Owen, spent the night because the next day was Owen's first birthday, and she recruited me to help her make the cake. When we were leaving my place to go to the birthday party, she made a trip out to her car with some stuff and left Owen with me for a few minutes until she came back, and we could all leave for the party together. Only 12 months old, Owen did not understand that his mother was, of course, coming right back to get him. All he knew was that she had walked out and left him with some tall, strange *Auslander* (foreigner). (At this point in our relationship, he knew me only as the person who has a ceiling fan. Every time his mom brought him to my apartment, he immediately fixed his gaze on the thing going round and round above him. Germans typically do not own ceiling fans.)

When his mom walked out of the building he started to cry: a natural response. As I held him and told him that everything was okay —that his MAMA would be right back—I realized something: the times in life when I cry are usually the times in which I am leaning on my insufficient, limited understanding. There have been so many times when I have been just like Owen, crying because I do not understand, because I cannot possibly comprehend that the hurt that I'm feeling is unnecessary. No one is hurting me or attempting to snatch away what I love. I am hurting only because I am refusing to trust God.

God is to me what I was to Owen that day. I held him tightly and reminded him that there was no need to cry. He was safe in my arms and regardless of whether his Mama came back or not (which of course she did), no harm was going to come to him unless I allowed it, and the only way I would allow him to hurt at all would be because it would ultimately bring him good that could not have been bestowed on him in any other way.

"Trust in the Lord with all your heart and lean not on your own understanding" (Proverbs 3:5). Why? Our understanding is as feeble as Owen's was that day.

Mary and Martha's understanding was also feeble and frail. "Let's never forget that some of His greatest mercies are His refusals. He says no in order that He may, in some way we cannot imagine, say yes. All His ways with us are merciful. His meaning is always love" (E. Elliot, Keep A Quiet Heart 118, 119). Jesus, of course, knew exactly what He was doing. He wanted to prove to the world that He was victorious over everything, even death. This was going to be a lesson his friends and enemies would do well to remember!

So He waited, and Lazarus died. He waited long enough to ensure that Lazarus was in the ground for several days. Everyone knew that Lazarus had died. Jesus was going to bring him back from the dead, and He wanted His glory to be spread far and wide. This is not an ordinary man; this is the Christ, the Son of God, the Resurrection and the Life!

On top of that, He was a true friend. When Mary wept, He wept too, even though He knew that Lazarus was soon to walk out of that tomb. He wept for his friends, He wept over their disappointment and hurt, He wept over their weak faith, and He wept because the time was soon approaching when He would have to leave them and face His own death.

Focus on verse 40 of John chapter11: "Then Jesus said, 'Did I not tell you that if you believe, you will see the glory of God?'" The glory of God is what God wants us to see. He could have come right away and healed Lazarus. Instead, he waited and miraculously raised Lazarus from the dead!

Jesus said, "if you believe . . ." Believe what? If you believe that I am who I say I am, that I am able to do what I say I am able to do, that my purposes are always loving, my character is always righteous and my intentions are always good, you will see the glory of God! Oh, if only we could choose to believe that instead of wallowing in our disappointment over what He doesn't do, or isn't doing. Oh, God, if we could only trust You! If only our hope could be in You alone!

And the dead man came out, his hands and feet wrapped with strips of linen, and a cloth around his face. Jesus said to them, "Take off the grave clothes and let him go." **The glory of God! I want to see**

**it, don't you? I want to see it more than I want to see my own desires realized!**

That is the lesson of Lazarus' death and resurrection. The will of God and the glory of God should be our number one desire. Lean not on your own understanding. In times when you are tempted to doubt God's goodness, choose instead to trust Him!

**THE DEATH OF JESUS**
**Matthew 27:22-66**

*"What shall I do, then, with Jesus who is called Christ?" Pilate asked.*

*They all answered, "Crucify him!"*

*"Why? What crime has he committed?" asked Pilate.*

*But they shouted all the louder, "Crucify him!"*

*When Pilate saw that he was getting nowhere, but that instead an uproar was starting, he took water and washed his hands in front of the crowd. "I am innocent of this man's blood," he said. "It is your responsibility!"*

*All the people answered, "Let his blood be on us and on our children!"*

*Then he released Barabbas to them. But he had Jesus flogged, and handed him over to be crucified.*

***The Soldiers Mock Jesus***

*Then the governor's soldiers took Jesus into the Praetorium and gathered the whole company of soldiers around him. They stripped him and put a scarlet robe on him, and then twisted together a crown of thorns and set it on his head. They put a staff in his right hand and knelt in front of him and mocked him. "Hail, king of the Jews!" they said. They spit on him, and took the staff and struck him on the head again and again. After they had mocked him, they took off the robe and put his own clothes on him. Then they led him away to crucify him.*

### *The Crucifixion*

*As they were going out, they met a man from Cyrene, named Simon, and they forced him to carry the cross. They came to a place called Golgotha (which means The Place of the Skull). There they offered Jesus wine to drink, mixed with gall; but after tasting it, he refused to drink it. When they had crucified him, they divided up his clothes by casting lots. And sitting down, they kept watch over him there. Above his head they placed the written charge against him: THIS IS JESUS, THE KING OF THE JEWS. Two robbers were crucified with him, one on his right and one on his left. Those who passed by hurled insults at him, shaking their heads and saying, "You who are going to destroy the temple and build it in three days, save yourself! Come down from the cross, if you are the Son of God!"*

*In the same way the chief priests, the teachers of the law and the elders mocked him. "He saved others," they said, "but he can't save himself! He's the King of Israel! Let him come down now from the cross, and we will believe in him. He trusts in God. Let God rescue him now if he wants him, for he said, 'I am the Son of God.' " In the same way the robbers who were crucified with him also heaped insults on him.*

### *The Death of Jesus*

*From the sixth hour until the ninth hour darkness came over all the land. About the ninth hour Jesus cried out in a loud voice, "Eloi, Eloi, lama sabachthani?"—which means, "My God, my God, why have you forsaken me?"*

*When some of those standing there heard this, they said, "He's calling Elijah."*

*Immediately one of them ran and got a sponge. He filled it with wine vinegar, put it on a stick, and offered it to Jesus to drink. The rest said, "Now leave him alone. Let's see if Elijah comes to save him."*

*And when Jesus had cried out again in a loud voice, he gave up his spirit.*

*At that moment the curtain of the temple was torn in two from top to bottom. The earth shook and the rocks split. The tombs broke open and the bodies of many holy people who had died were raised to life. They came out of the tombs, and after Jesus' resurrection they went into the holy city and appeared to many people.*

*When the centurion and those with him who were guarding Jesus saw the earthquake and all that had happened, they were terrified, and exclaimed, "Surely he was the Son of God!"*

*Many women were there, watching from a distance. They had followed Jesus from Galilee to care for his needs. Among them were Mary Magdalene, Mary the mother of James and Joses, and the mother of Zebedee's sons.*

### *The Burial of Jesus*

*As evening approached, there came a rich man from Arimathea, named Joseph, who had himself become a disciple of Jesus. Going to Pilate, he asked for Jesus' body, and Pilate ordered that it be given to him. Joseph took the body, wrapped it in a clean linen cloth, and placed it in his own new tomb that he had cut out of the rock. He rolled a big stone in front of the entrance to the tomb and went away. Mary Magdalene and the other Mary were sitting there opposite the tomb.*

### *The Guard at the Tomb*

*The next day, the one after Preparation Day, the chief priests and the Pharisees went to Pilate. "Sir," they said, "we remember that while he was still alive that deceiver said, 'After three days I will rise again.' So give the order for the tomb to be made secure until the third day. Otherwise, his disciples may come and steal the body and tell the people that he has been raised from the dead. This last deception will be worse than the first."*

*"Take a guard," Pilate answered. "Go, make the tomb as secure as you know how." So they went and made the tomb secure by putting a seal on the stone and posting the guard.*

The Son of God was dead. We cannot imagine the extreme disappointment and grief that was felt by Jesus' mother, Mary, and all of his friends and followers, because they did not yet understand. The same man who had raised Lazarus from the dead was now dead himself.

**The Resurrection**
**Matthew 28:1-6**

*After the Sabbath, at dawn on the first day of the week, Mary Magdalene and the other Mary went to look at the tomb.*

*There was a violent earthquake, for an angel of the Lord came down from heaven and, going to the tomb, rolled back the stone and sat on it. His appearance was like lightning, and his clothes were white as snow. The guards were so afraid of him that they shook and became like dead men.*

*The angel said to the women, "Do not be afraid, for I know that you are looking for Jesus, who was crucified. He is not here; he has risen, just as he said.*

Without this story, our entire lives would be disappointments: meaningless, hopeless, purposeless, lifeless, but HE HAS RISEN, JUST AS HE SAID! There is meaning, there is hope, there is purpose, there is life! Praise God!

**DEATH WITH CHRIST IS HOPE!**

I work with a church planting team. One week I had the opportunity to visit another vibrant, little church plant in a different part of the city. The pastor had this to say about the cross: "When we are dead at the cross, we anticipate resurrection. When we are alive at the cross, we expect disappointment." He is expressing what Paul expressed in Romans 6:6, 8: "For we know that our old self was crucified with him . . . Now if we died with Christ, we believe that we will also live with Him." The cross of Christ is our Hope! If we died with Christ, if we were crucified with him and buried with him, we are also raised to Life with Him! Death with Christ is HOPE . . . it is the definition of Hope! Death apart from Christ is just the opposite; it is hopelessness.

If a person dies physically, and he or she did not possess faith in Christ ("For it is by grace you have been saved, through faith" Ephesians 2:8), he or she dies a hopeless death. Death apart from

Christ is hopeless. There is no hope. However, if a person who is "in Christ" dies, death is all about hope! "If only for this life we have hope in Christ, we are of all people most to be pitied" (1 Corinthians 15:19). Our hope is also for the *next* life! Death is simply a gateway.

> *Then the end will come, when he hands over the kingdom to God the Father after he has destroyed all dominion, authority and power. For he must reign until he has put all his enemies under his feet. The last enemy to be destroyed is death. . . "Death has been swallowed up in victory." "Where, O death, is your victory? Where, O death, is your sting?" The sting of death is sin, and the power of sin is the law. But thanks be to God! He gives us the victory through our Lord Jesus Christ (1 Corinthians 15:24-26, 54b-57).*

If death is overwhelming you, and it feels like God could not possibly be loving and take from you someone you love, remember that God Himself gave His only Son over to death on a cross so that we might LIVE, even though we die. Look to the cross to understand victory over death. Look to the cross to understand love. "For God so loved the world that he gave his one and only Son . . ." (John 3:16).

Rufinus explained the cross as being the height and breadth and depth of "the love of Christ" (Ephesians 3:18). "The part which is fixed in the earth he calls the 'depth,' that which is erected upon the earth and reaches upward is the 'height,' and that which is spread out to the right hand and to the left is the 'breadth'" (Rufinus). To understand the depth and height and breadth of the love of Christ is to understand the cross!

"O that old rugged cross, so despised by the world, has a wondrous attraction for me" (Bennard). Paul prayed that the Ephesians, being rooted and established in love, may have power to grasp the cross. Oh to be so rooted in the love of God!

You may have noticed that all three of the biblical stories in this chapter have something glaringly obvious in common, something which may, at first glance, diminish the comfort we so desperately seek. They all end with the person who died being restored to life. I need to say something about this before I go on: this is only possible with Jesus.

Physical life has a time limit. There is no way around that. My grandpa died of kidney failure when my mom was a junior in high school. I never had the privilege of meeting him. Both of my sisters-in-law have miscarried, meaning two of my nephews or nieces will never be a part of our lives on earth. Since I moved to Germany, two of my grandparents have passed away. Friends of our family have died of cancer, ALS, heart attacks, etc. There is no escaping death.

Here is a verse I want to highlight and leave with you. **Jesus said, "I am the resurrection and the life. The one who believes in me will live, even though they die"** (John 11:25). Death is certain and our days are ordained, or appointed (Psalm 139:16) but even though we will die physically, we can live for eternity because of Christ! Each death can end in resurrection! That is why I am a missionary.

What about those we love who have died without faith in Christ? Or what about people who never heard about Christ? In my job, I am asked these questions often. Here is my answer: don't waste time worrying about people's destinies, as that is God's job; instead, be part of the solution.

> *Then Jesus came to them and said, "All authority in heaven and on earth has been given to me. Therefore go and make disciples of all nations, baptizing them in the name of the Father and of the Son and of the Holy Spirit, and teaching them to obey everything I have commanded you. And surely I am with you always, to the very end of the age" (Matthew 28:18-20).*

Do not waste your disappointment; redeem it, and transform it into an APPOINTMENT!

**DEATH**

Discussion Questions

1. Have you experienced the death of someone you love? How did it feel to walk through that disappointment?

2. What, if anything, brought you comfort during or after the passing of a loved one?

3. How does the death of Jesus bring you comfort?

4. Life on earth is short. What do you think God wants us to accomplish during our fleeting lives?

5. Death is certain and our days are ordained, or appointed (Psalm 139:16) but even though we will die physically, we can live for eternity because of Christ! How can one be assured of eternal life?

6. If eternal life is obtained through faith in Christ, how active should we be in sharing Christ with others?

# CHAPTER SEVEN
# APPOINTED

*"When you are disappointed, examine yourself to make certain you are thinking and living in harmony with God's purpose. It could be that you have wandered off the Godly path. Instead of dwelling upon the word "disappointment," think of it as "God-appointment." What you regard as a disappointment may actually be a wonderful new plan for your life—namely, HIS plan."*

**Norman Vincent Peale**

This book is primarily about dis-appointment, but have you ever thought about the fact that you have been APPOINTED? You were appointed:

- To life and breath
- To a time period
- To a nation or land

*And he is not served by human hands, as if he needed anything. Rather, he himself gives everyone* ***life and breath*** *and everything else. From one man he made all the nations, that they should inhabit the whole earth; and he marked out their* ***APPOINTED times*** *in history and* ***the boundaries of their lands****. God did this so that they would seek him and perhaps reach out for him and find him, though he is not far from any one of us (Acts 17:25-27).*

- To an earthly family
- To a body type, a personality, a skill set, strengths & weaknesses
- To a number of days on earth

*For you created* ***my inmost being****; you knit me together in my mother's womb. I praise you because* ***I am fearfully and wonderfully made****; your works are wonderful, I know that full well. My frame was not hidden from you when I was made in the secret place, when I was woven together in the depths of the earth. Your eyes saw my unformed body;* ***all the days ORDAINED for me*** *were written in your book before one of them came to be (Psalm 139:13-16).*

- To God
- To spiritual blessings in Christ
- To be holy and blameless
- To be adopted as sons and daughters to a heavenly family!
- To redemption (salvation) through his blood
- To forgiveness
- To eternal life

*Praise be to the God and Father of our Lord Jesus Christ, who has blessed us in the heavenly realms with* ***every spiritual blessing*** *in Christ. For he* ***CHOSE US*** *in him before the creation* *of the world to be **holy** and **blameless** in his sight. In love he **PREDESTINED US for adoption to sonship** through Jesus Christ, in accordance with his pleasure and will—to the praise of his glorious grace, which he has freely given us in the One he loves. In him we have **redemption** through his blood, the forgiveness of sins. . . (Ephesians 1:3-7a).*

*For this is what the Lord has commanded us: 'I have made you a light for the Gentiles, that you may bring **salvation** to the ends of the earth.' When the Gentiles heard this, they were glad and honored the word of the Lord; and all who were **APPOINTED** for **eternal life** believed" (Acts 13:47-48).*

- To an inheritance
- To sufferings
- To glory

*The Spirit himself testifies with our spirit that we are God's children. Now if we are children, then **we are heirs**—heirs of God and co-heirs with Christ, if indeed we share in his **sufferings** in order that we may also share in his **glory** (Romans 8:16, 17).*

- To good works
- To bear fruit

*For we are God's handiwork, created in Christ Jesus to do **good works**, which God **PREPARED IN ADVANCE** for us to do (Ephesians 2:10).*

*You did not choose me, but I **CHOSE YOU** and **APPOINTED** you so that you might go and **bear fruit**—fruit that will last. . . (John 15:16a).*

- To die

*And as it is **APPOINTED** unto men once **to die**, but after this the judgment . . . (Hebrews 9:27 KJV).*

Finally, we are appointed to die. The day will come. Until then though, we must live and live for Christ! The Apostle Paul penned these incredible words:

> *For to me, to live is Christ and to die is gain. If I am to go on living in the body, this will mean fruitful labor for me. Yet what shall I choose? I do not know! I am torn between the two: I desire to depart and be with Christ, which is better by far; but it is more necessary for you that I remain in the body. Convinced of this, I know that I will remain, and I will continue with all of you for your progress and joy in the faith . . . (Philippians 1:21-25).*

To die is gain! Living, though, must mean fruitful labor, and that is hard Kingdom work!

You should have all the biblical proof you now need to fully, whole-heartedly believe that God does not disappoint His children, but He appoints them! Earthly fathers can and do disappoint us, but the same is not true of our heavenly Father. It is not a matter of perspective; it is a matter of correct theology. Let me be clear: God is involved in our losses, our heartbreaks, our grief, our hardships, but He appoints us to these things, not to hurt us or to crush us, but to GROW and mature us.

> *And not only this, but we also exult in our tribulations, knowing that tribulation brings about perseverance and perseverance, proven character; and proven character, hope; and hope does not disappoint, because the love of God has been poured out within our hearts through the Holy Spirit who was given to us (Romans 5:3-5, NASB).*

A few years ago, friends and I took a road trip to southern Germany. On the way back to Berlin we came upon a yellow sign that read, "Umleitung," the German word for detour. This detour wound us around country roads for probably 45 minutes before we found our way back to the Autobahn that we had left. A couple of times, we drove for 10-15 minutes before seeing another "Umleitung" sign letting us know that we were, in fact, still correctly following the detour. It was a confusing and exasperating experience, especially since we were all hungry and in need of restrooms.

This little anecdote showed me something that I had never realized before. Many times in life, we chart our own course and are then shocked, frustrated, confused and even angry when the road we wanted to take is suddenly not a possibility. I have hit many "detours" already in life but have labeled them "disappointments," which I've found is usually an error in judgment. Most of life's "disappointments" are APPOINTMENTS from God Himself!

Detours should not be looked upon as negative turns of events, but as God's guidance. "For my thoughts are not your thoughts, neither are your ways my ways," declares the LORD. "As the heavens are higher than the earth, so are my ways higher than your ways and my thoughts than your thoughts" (Isaiah 55:8,9). Praise God when, in His great wisdom, He redirects your path saving you from unseen heartache and even destruction. It may mean a delay or even a stand-still, but trust God—there is a reason!

## JOSEPH'S APPOINTMENT

No story proves this point more than the account of Joseph in the book of Genesis. After being favored by his father (which caused his brothers to be jealous and hate him), thrown into a cistern and sold into slavery, reported as dead to his father, bought by Midianite merchants, re-sold to Potiphar, falsely accused of sinning with Potiphar's wife and imprisoned in a dungeon for years, he was FINALLY **appointed** to be "in charge of the whole land of Egypt" (Genesis 41:41). "Joseph was thirty years old when he entered the service of Pharaoh king of Egypt" (v. 46), and he went on to save the land, as well as his family, from a severe famine. Quite an appointment for such a young man!

You see, Joseph was appointed exactly like we are: to life, to a time period in history, to a nation, to an earthly family, to skills and strengths, to a number of days on earth, to God, to sufferings, and to specific good works which God prepared in advance for him to do! There SEEMED to be many, many disappointments or detours in his story, but it is crystal clear all these generations later that he was appointed to be used of God for God's purpose and glory. We are appointed, just like Joseph was, to be used of God for God's purposes and glory.

## MY APPOINTMENT

Generations ago, in the year 1865, my great, great, great grandparents on my mother's side, Joseph and Mary Warneka, emigrated from Berlin, Germany (then Prussia) and settled near Waterloo, Iowa where they were members of the Lutheran church. Their son, my great, great grandfather, August, came over on the ship with his parents at the age of six. August married Viva and they had three children, including my great grandpa Clarence. Clarence married Edith, and my grandma Helen was the last of their five children.

Clarence and Edith came to faith at an evangelistic rally in Waterloo with Billy Sunday. The year was 1932 and Billy's daughter had just died, so devastating Billy that he told his wife, Nell, "he didn't think he could go on preaching. Nell asked him what he wanted to do and Billy couldn't answer. He kept his next speaking engagement in Waterloo, Iowa" (Bruns 292). It was at that meeting that my great grandparents understood and embraced Christ's sacrifice. Billy Sunday understood a little something of turning disappointment into an appointment, and my family has been forever impacted. A few years later, my grandma came to know and trust Christ at age 13 sitting under the preaching at Walnut Street Baptist Church in Waterloo, where her parents had begun attending.

My grandma married Burton Bartling on April 23, 1948. Here is his testimony in his own words:

> *I shall never forget how God led that I might be saved. It starts with my entering the service in 1942. I tried joining the Marines at the Induction Center, but my teeth held me back. I'm sure God was leading even then. Before long our Army training was completed, and overseas we went. I remember plainly the fear of what was ahead. The next two years was continuous strain of fear—then the war ended. My next problem was great—what is my future? I really depended on friends at home for help. Soon I discovered people at home were not capable of helping a fellow all mixed up from the war. Consequently, God provided that a missionary should be visiting her mother in our home town. She was waiting for acceptance for passage on a plane to Africa. This missionary knew my friend, and through him I met her. Immediately she knew my need. I accepted Christ a month after*

*being out of the service. Truly I can say God works in lives. People prayed for my salvation.*

He went on to attend Grace Theological Seminary and then established First Baptist Church of Argus, Indiana before returning to Waterloo.

As a result, my mom grew up in a Christian home. My grandpa, her dad, died on November 6, 1971, at the age of 48, leaving my grandma a widow with six children. My grandma turned her disappointment into an appointment and raised her children, as best as she could, to go on for God.

My mom met my dad at Bible college in Clarks Summit, Pennsylvania. They married in 1976, and my dad entered the ministry as a youth pastor in Ypsilanti, Michigan. I was born on January 8, 1978. We moved to Ankeny, Iowa when I was five, and it was there that I believed in Christ, was baptized, and decided to become a missionary when I grew up.

My family background explains how special an appointment it is that I grew up in Iowa and later became a missionary in Berlin, Germany. Talk about life coming full circle! Almost 150 years later, I am back in the land of my Lutheran ancestors, as a single missionary like the one who led my grandpa to Christ, church planting like my grandpa and reaching teenagers like my dad. God is an author of beautiful stories, full of heartaches, but even more full of His grace and purpose!

**APPOINTED**
Discussion Questions

1. We've taken a long look at our disappointments. Let's look specifically now at your appointments!

   To when did God appoint you to be born?

   Where did He appoint you to live?

   Why did He appoint you to live in this specific time period in this specific place? See Acts 17:25-27.

   To which family did He appoint you? Why do you think He chose your family for you?

   Briefly describe the body type, personality, skill set, strengths & weaknesses to which God appointed you?

   What are the specific good works that God prepared in advance for YOU to do? What "fruit" did He appoint YOU to bear?

2. What disappointments can you begin to see as appointments from God?

3. Why would God not disappoint His children?

# CHAPTER EIGHT
# TIMING

*"We are not dealing with a genie in a bottle;*
*we are dealing with Almighty God."*
**Steve Dye, pastor**

*"Supposedly God answers every prayer with a 'yes', 'no', or 'wait,',*
*but for me it seems like He only says, 'no' or 'wait a really, really,*
*really long time!'"*
**A friend**

*"My soul is in deep anguish. How long, LORD, how long? Turn,*
*LORD, and deliver me; save me because of your unfailing love."*
**Psalm 6:3**

*"How long, LORD? Will you forget me forever? How long will you*
*hide your face from me? How long must I wrestle with my thoughts*
*and day after day have sorrow in my heart? How long will my enemy*
*triumph over me?"*
**Psalm 13:1-2**

*"Since ancient times, no one has heard, no ear has perceived,*
*no eye has seen any God besides you, who acts on behalf of those*
*who wait for him."*
**Isaiah 64:4**

I read through my old journals recently, from up to 10 years ago, and it catapulted me into severe disappointment with God. I was suddenly faced with evidence of years of unfulfilled hopes and seemingly unanswered prayers. There it was right in front of me: dreams, desires, and pleas in my own handwriting, and all these years later they were still unrealized. One of the greatest "disappointments" in life is that of God's timing. I do not consider myself an angry person, but the times I am are usually a result of what I presume or assess to be God's slowness or apathy. Reading through my old journals was one of those angry times with God, one of those times that could have led me on a path away from Him. This was the prayer I penned shortly after that spiritual "valley":

## I DON'T WANT THIS APPOINTMENT

*God, I realize you appoint, not disappoint, but I don't want this appointment anymore. I'm tired of putting on my mask and cape and being superwoman. I'm tired of faking bravery. I'm tired of doing it all alone.*

*I don't understand why you don't answer my prayers, or rather why Your answer is always "no" or "wait." It's been a decade of praying this same prayer. I try to pray in faith without doubting, but I can barely even talk to You about this anymore because I feel like we've had this same conversation a thousand times and it always ends the same way. With silence.*

*Getting to approach the throne of Almighty God is such a privilege, but it feels lonely in the Throne Room. I don't hear anything but my own voice. I wish instead You could be sitting with me here at this table in this coffee shop and actually be audibly conversing with me. Instead, I am waiting for two teenage girls to show up so I can talk with them about baptism. Again, it feels like it's just me, but You promised that if I was about the Great Commission, You would be with me always. You promised in Mark's Gospel that if I left home and country and family for the sake of the Gospel, You would replace it all a hundred times over. But I'm so often alone, in a foreign country, reaching people for You.*

*I need You, God. I need to sense You, to hear You, to see Your answers to my prayers. I need to see You accomplish above and beyond what I ask or even imagine. Instead it seems like I'm always asking for more than You're willing to give.*

That is raw honesty from the heart of an unmarried missionary. It is hard and, at times, the road feels long and far too quiet. In these times when our human wills battle with the will of God, we need to remember those who have gone before us. Every person who has ever lived and had sincere faith in God has gone through similar valleys (read Hebrews 11), but just as life cannot be lived entirely on the mountaintop, life is not lived entirely in the valley. From the valley, I look up to the mountains and say, "Why God? Why do I have to be down here instead of up there? I've been down here so long." And into the silence He speaks, if I am willing to be silent enough to listen.

## WAITING

"I want to take you to the mountaintop, but you are not yet ready. The climb is hard and steep and you must train a while longer. This valley is preparing you. Suffering and waiting produce the necessary perseverance, character and hope that you will need to get to the top, without which you would certainly fail. Trust me. It seems to you too long, but it is a necessary amount of time. My timing is perfect. I have not forgotten you. I see your faithfulness and your struggle. I appreciate your honesty. I am with you always, and soon, when you are ready, we will stand on the summit together, and when you look back down on that valley, you will finally understand."

Waiting and trust are issues so key, so integral to the topic of disappointment that they deserve their own chapter. Trust in God and contentment are choices. They are not forced upon us, but unless we choose them daily, we WILL be miserable. The "disappointments" of life will choke out joy. I know many miserable people who are miserable simply of their own accord. They have *chosen* misery, and misery is like a dark cloud that keeps us from seeing the sun; the even scarier truth is that misery is not an end in and of itself. Misery is a road, and that road will lead us away from God and cause us to miss out on His blessings.

In Deuteronomy chapter one, Moses describes a time when God's people missed His blessings because of their perceived disappointment with God. Moses delivered a message from God to the people of Israel that it was time to leave Horeb and go "take possession of the land" (v. 8) the LORD had promised to Abraham, Isaac and Jacob. They sent out 12 spies, "one man from each tribe" (v. 23) to go ahead of the people, explore the land and bring back a report. The report that came back was positive: "It is a good land that the Lord our God is giving us" (v. 25), but the people refused to go. They grumbled and said, "The LORD hates us; so he brought us out of Egypt . . . to destroy us. . . The people are stronger and taller than we are; the cities are large, with walls up to the sky" (v. 27-28). Do you hear the misery in the words, "The LORD hates us?" They were like children having a temper tantrum.

Despite exhortation and reminders from Moses that they did not need to be terrified, that the LORD would fight for them, they did not trust in the LORD their God. As a result, that generation did not enter the Promised Land of Canaan. After forty years in the wilderness, with God miraculously supplying for their needs every step of the way, they chose the road of misery instead of the road of blessing. They missed the Promised Land. God's timing took too long. They wanted instant gratification instead of delayed blessings, and the choice to be miserable won over. They missed it. Moreover, Moses also missed it because of their devastatingly poor choices. You see, friends, our choice to be miserable never affects only us.

Don't miss God's blessings! John 1:16 tells us that, "From his abundance we have all received one gracious blessing after another." Another translation says it this way, "For from his fullness we have all received, grace upon grace" (ESV).

I remember clearly one beautiful summer vacation with my family on Lake Michigan. I stood one day on the shore with my toes in the wet sand, reflecting on God's grace as the gentle waves lapped up onto the beach one after another. God's goodness is like those waves: "one gracious blessing after another," over and over for the rest of our lives. Psalm 23:6 so beautifully promises, "Surely goodness and mercy shall follow me all the days of my life."

We can easily miss it in our disappointment with God's timing. My journals, and my recent reaction to them, are evidence of how much I struggle with God's timing in my life. However, I choose joy! I will not choose misery. I will be honest about my struggle with God's will and timing, but I consciously make the choice to trust Him and I want to make this choice every single day of my life, because He is good. His grace is an outpouring of His abundance. His blessings are unending. He anoints my head with oil; my cup overflows (Psalm 23:5). To miss it all would be irrevocably, irreversibly foolish, and all we have to do to miss it is focus on perceived injustice instead.

Very recently, I went on a trip to Albania to help out at a training and encouragement retreat for missionaries serving in the Balkan Peninsula (Bulgaria, Bosnia, Kosovo, etc.). While there, I met a lady who is now a hero of mine. Her name is Nadine Hennesey. You need to read her book, *When You Don't See His Plan: The Nadine Hennesey Story*. I won't ruin it for you, but she is an example of someone who could have easily missed God's blessings because of misery, but she didn't. The wisdom I gained from meeting her and reading her story is invaluable, similar to reading books by Elisabeth Elliot. These women did not miss it. They got it, and I want to be like them, counted among the number in Hebrews chapter 11 "whose weakness was turned to strength" (v. 34), who were "commended for their faith" (v. 39). I want to persevere because I see "him who is invisible" (v. 27)

His timing will never be mine, of that I am sure. I always want what I want immediately. I hate waiting, but I feel like it is all I do. I wait for public transportation, for financial provision, for people, for Wi-Fi to work at cafes, for responses to emails . . . but in reality the world has never moved faster. It used to take weeks to cross the Atlantic. It takes me less than 10 hours. Fifty to sixty years ago, people living abroad waited weeks to receive letters in the mail from friends and family back home. Now we access information the moment it happens. When my nieces and nephews were born, I found out within minutes thanks to the internet.

The problem is that this fast-paced, digital, instant-gratification world we live in has diminished our ability to wait. Patience is not a virtue many possess. It is a real problem for me and a reason that I struggle so badly with God's timing. I have to remember that there are just as many blessings in the waiting room as there are in the actual appointment. There were just as many blessings in the wilderness as there would be in the Promised Land. Don't miss it. Open your eyes. "From his abundance we have all received one gracious blessing after another" (John 1:16 NLT). The valley, the mountaintop, the wilderness, the promised land . . . His grace is there. HE is there! His timing is not a disappointment and He CERTAINLY is not a disappointment!

My new prayer is this:

*God, I want this appointment. It is from You, and though it seems often like a wilderness, it has been full of blessings, full of Your grace, full of Your answers, full of Your presence! I want it, Lord. I want anything and everything You have for me because You are good and You are love and Your plans and timing are for my good, for my sanctification, for Your glory. I choose to wait on You. I choose to trust.*

**TIMING**

Discussion Questions

1. What are the still-unanswered prayers for you right now? Have they gone unanswered long enough that they are causing you to struggle with disappointment with God?

2. Do you feel you are in the valley or on the mountaintop right now? Why?

3. Recall a time in life when you were miserable and discontent. (Perhaps it is right now.) Do you think you missed out on God's blessings during that time?

4. List His grace and blessings in your life this week. Take sufficient time to list as many as you can!

5. Can you say that you want the appointments God has for you right now? If not, how can you seek to transform and renew your mind to joyfully accept His will?

# CHAPTER NINE
# HOPE

*"A week passed, and no news arrived of Mr. Rochester: ten days; and still he did not come. Mrs. Fairfax said she should not be surprised if he were to . . . not show his face again at Thornfield for a year . . . When I heard this I was beginning to feel a strange chill and failing at the heart. I was actually permitting myself to experience a sickening sense of disappointment . . . Every good, true, vigorous feeling I have, gathers impulsively round him. I know I must conceal my sentiments: I must smother hope . . ."*

**Charlotte Brontë • Jane Eyre**

*Why, my soul, are you downcast? Why so disturbed within me? Put your hope in God, for I will yet praise him, my Savior and my God.*

**Psalm 42:5, 11, 43:5, NIV**

*Now hope does not disappoint, because the love of God has been poured out in our hearts by the Holy Spirit who was given to us.*

**Romans 5:5, NKJV**

*"I am the LORD; those who hope in me will not be disappointed."*

**Isaiah 49:23b, NIV**

Hope and disappointment are directly linked. In regard to disappointment, hope is both the problem and the solution. It is because hope exists that we can be disappointed. Remember my definition of disappointment from chapter one?

**Kristi's Definition of Disappointment**—an unfulfilled self-appointment, expectation, longing, desire, or hope in someone or something other than God and His will, resulting in feelings of loss, sadness, or even depression.

Keep that in mind while you use your imagination for a moment. Imagine yourself sick with disappointment; so sick that you are physically aching. Now imagine yourself in the waiting room of a doctor's office. You are tempted to flip through a magazine to pass the time, but your nerves will not let you. You haven't slept, you haven't eaten. You are shaky and weak. Finally, the nurse calls your name. You walk apprehensively to the examining room. After seemingly endless minutes, the doctor enters and you describe your symptoms: insomnia, nausea, inability to focus, lack of energy, depression, stress headaches, possibly even suicidal thoughts. The doctor jots some notes on your chart, occasionally nodding and responding with "mmhhm." Finally he pulls out his prescription pad, scribbles a word, rips off the page and hands it to you. The page simply reads "Hope."

*Hope? That is not a medicine. You cannot swallow it or let it dissolve under your tongue. No pharmacist will fill this prescription! It's useless. Plus, isn't unfulfilled hope the reason I am in here in the first place?!*

You wad up the paper and throw it back at the physician. *Here, you keep your hope! I need something a LOT more effective!*

But there is nothing stronger than hope, is there? Hope has been called "an anchor" (Hebrews 6:19), "a pillar" and "a waking dream" (Pliny the Elder), and "the thing with feathers that perches in the soul" (Emily Dickinson).

*There is no medicine like hope, no incentive so great, and no tonic so powerful as expectation of something better tomorrow.*
-Orison S. Marden (Chang 281)

*Don't you know that day dawns after night, showers displace drought, and spring and summer follow winter? Then, have*

*hope! Hope forever, for God will not fail you!*
-Charles Spurgeon (qtd. in S. Young xii)

*Of all ills that one endures, hope is a cheap and universal cure.*
-Abraham Cowley (Johnson 69)

*What gives me the most hope every day is God's grace; knowing that his grace is going to give me the strength for whatever I face, knowing that nothing is a surprise to God.*
-Rick Warren (qtd. in Supen 49)

But hope, like belief, love, and desire, must have an object. Hope that is not *in* something is nothing. **There is an even bigger danger than a hope in nothing; that is a hope in something that can fail. For instead of being a cure for disappointment, it is now the catalyst for even more manifold disappointment!** We constantly hope in people, dreams, ideas, theories, institutions, inventions, the newest diet plan, the latest fad, whatever is currently "trending" or circulating on social media. We jump at articles offering "secrets" to boost happiness, slash grocery bills, lower blood pressure, simplify life, reduce stress, control weight, curb the appetite, spice up marriage, and regain our lives. We are so willing and ready to hope . . . but in what? When we have problems, we turn to Google, scan Pinterest for a creative solution, or petition our Facebook friends, usually before we ever turn to God.

It's all about a quick fix and instant gratification, but quick and instant solutions usually last as long as cotton candy; satisfying for a brief moment in time. A good book and a caramel macchiato distract me from small disappointments and soothe my frazzled nerves for as long as I am in the coffee shop. Often that rest and reprieve from the stress of daily life does truly help, but it is like a Band-Aid on a soul wound. That wound we are calling disappointment needs a more permanent repair or it will reopen and fester time and time again. **A serious disappointment, if left unattended with only a Band-Aid type solution, has the potential to develop into the gangrene of bitterness!** This is because of unfulfilled hope in something other than God and His will.

Returning to the story of the Shunammite woman from 2 Kings 4 proves the danger of what I have termed "false hope." The full story is found in chapter five, but I want to focus on verse 28: "Did I ask you for a son, my lord?" she said. "Didn't I tell you, 'Don't raise my hopes'?" (NIV). To raise our own hopes or even someone else's is very dangerous if those hopes are in something we are not sure is the will of God.

We must learn the difference between the temporary and the eternal, the finite and the infinite, the unreliable and the dependable. That kind of happiness is fleeting; here today and gone tomorrow.

In Bible college I began reading the works of Elisabeth Elliot, and quickly grew to love her. Reading through her stories and journal entries taught me to put my trust and hope in God alone because everything else is unsure. She spent years waiting on her first love, Jim, to finally propose, and then they were only married a brief two years before he was murdered by the same people he was attempting to reach with the Gospel. If her hope had been in Jim or romantic love, she would have been lost. Since Christ was her hope, she not only survived the passing of her young husband, but she went on to thrive as she continued his work with the Huaorani people.

Hope in God is THE answer for disappointment: hope that God is good, hope that He cares, hope that He is sovereign and wise, hope that He loved us to the point of sending His Son to die for our sins, hope that He delights in doing the impossible, hope that His grace is enough for every circumstance, hope that heaven (eternity with God) awaits all who trust in His salvation, hope that He is coming again! This kind of hope is CERTAIN! It is TRUE! It is the cure for, and the protection from, disappointment.

**HOPE**
Discussion Questions

1. How are hope and disappointment linked?

2. What does Kristi believe is an even greater danger than a hope in nothing?

3. What is the difference between false hope and true hope?

4. What is the cure for disappointment?

5. Is your hope in God? How do you know?

Dear Reader,

I thank you for going on this journey with me. I am glad, for your sake and mine, that the reason I began writing this book is still my reality. I am still single, and it is still difficult. In the seven+ years it has taken me to write this book, my circumstances have not changed, and I'm glad. I'm glad because I can pen these final words out of the angst and honesty of being still "in the struggle." My desire is still unfulfilled, but my perspective has changed. My hope used to be in the fulfillment of this desire, and now, more and more often, it is in God and His will for my life, whatever that may be. Singleness has become much less of a *disappointment* and much more of an *appointment*! You see, it is possible to experience fewer disappointments. It does not mean that we have to expect less, or expect nothing. We simply need to transfer our expectations and hope from uncertain things to HIM who is absolutely certain!

Hope in God, my friend. He will not disappoint you.

Sincerely,
Kristi
May 2015

"I am soon going off from this country, and will leave you to the care of him who neither slumbers nor sleeps, and never disappointed anyone who put his trust in him. If you make him your friend, he will be better to you than any companion can be. He is a friend that sticketh closer than a brother. May he grant you grace to seek him and to serve him. I have nothing better to say to you than to take God for your Father, Jesus for your Savior, and the Holy Spirit for your sanctifier" (David Livingstone, qtd. in Speer 11-12).

# Works Cited

"Arabah." n.d. *Visual Bible Alive*. Web. 2 October 2014. <http://www.visualbiblealive.com/resources.php?+category_id=4&encyc_id=594&img_id=29668&action=encyclopedia&frame=divEncyc>.

Ashworth, Crista. *Walking Your Child Through Disappointment*. 14 August 2014. 2 October 2014. <http://www.graceformoms.com/walking-child-disappointment/>.

Barlow, Tom. "15 Useful Items With a Lifetime Warranty." 27 June 2011. *Forbes*. Forbes Magazine. Web. 2 October 2014.

Bennard, George. "The Old Rugged Cross." Public Domain, 1913.

Benton, Michael. *Death of Benjamin Franklin*. 26 November 2013. Venturio Media Web Property. Web. 2 October 2014.

Brontë, Charlotte. "Jane Eyre." Penguin Books, 1960, 1982. Print.

Bruns, Roger A. *Preacher: Billy Sunday and Big-time American Evangelism*. New York: W. W. Norton, 1992. Print.

Chandra A, Copen CE, Stephen EH. *Infertility and impaired fecundity in the United States, 1982–2010: Data from the National Survey of Family Growth*. National health statistics reports; no 67. Hyattsville, MD: National Center for Health Statistics. 2013. PDF File.

Chang, Larry. *Wisdom for the Soul: Five Millennia of Prescriptions for Spiritual Healing*. Washington, D.C.: Gnosophia, 2006. Print.

*Charlotte Brontë*. n.d. Goodreads Inc. Web. 2 October 2014. <http://www.goodreads.com/author/quotes/1036615.Charlotte_Bront_>.

*Deborah Moggach Quotes (Author of the Best Exotic Marigold Hotel)*. n.d. Goodreads Inc. Web. 2 October 2014. <http://www.goodreads.com/author/quotes/41207.Deborah_Moggach>.

"Disappointment." n.d. *The Free Dictionary*. Farlex. Web. 2 October 2014. <http://www.thefreedictionary.com/disappointment>.

Eldredge, John. *Dare to Desire: An Invitation to Fulfill Your Deepest Dreams*. Nashville, TN: J. Countryman, 2002. Print.

Elliot, Elisabeth. *Keep A Quiet Heart*. Ann Arbor, MI: Vine, 1995. Print.

Elliot, Elisabeth. *Through Gates of Splendor*. Tyndale House Publishers, Inc., Copyright 1956, 1957, 1981. Print.

*Emily Dickinson Quotes*. n.d. Goodreads Inc. Web. 29 April 2015. <http://www.goodreads.com/quotes/5920-hope-is-the-thing-with-feathers-that-perches-in-the>.

Johnson, Samuel. *The Works of the Poets of Great Britain and Ireland*. London: A. Miller, 1800. Print.

Keller, Timothy J. *Walking with God through Pain and Suffering*. Penguin Group, 2013. Print.

Kreider, Rose M., and Tavia Simmons. *Marital Status, 2000*. Washington, D.C.: U.S. Dept. of Commerce, Economics and Statistics Administration, U.S. Census Bureau, 2003. PDF File.

Lewis, C. S. *The Four Loves*. New York: Harcourt Brace, 1960. Print.

Lewis, C. C. *The Great Divorce*. New York: Macmillan, 1946. Print.

Lucado, Max. *Traveling Light: Releasing the Burdens You Were Never Intended to Bear*. Nashville: W Group, 2001. Print.

Martindale, Wayne. *The Quotable Lewis*. Ed. Jerry Root. Wheaton: Tyndale House, 1989. Print.

Montgomery, Lucy Maud. *Anne of Green Gables*. Mogul, 2014. Print.

Morrow, T. G. *Christian Courtship in an Oversexed World*. Catholic Faith Alive!, Inc.; 2 edition, 2013. Print.

Peale, Norman Vincent. *Turn Disappointment to God-Appointment*. n.d. Web. 11 May 2015. <https://www.guideposts.org/faith/bible-resources/turn-disappointment-to-god-appointment>.

Picoult, Jodi. *My Sister's Keeper*. New York: Atria, 2004. Print.

Piper, John. *The Roots of Endurance: Invincible Perseverance in the Lives of John Newton, Charles Simeon, and William Wilberforce*. Wheaton: Crossway, 2002. Print.

Piper, John. *What Do Answers to Prayer Depend On? Part 2*. 25 January 1981. Web. 2 October 2014.

*Pliny the Elder Quotes*. n.d. BrainyQuote. Web. 29 April 2015. <http://www.brainyquote.com/quotes/quotes/p/plinytheel134956.html>.

Robinson, Robert. "Come, Thou Fount of Every Blessing." *John Wyeth's Repository of Sacred Music*. 1813. Print.

Rufinus. *Early Church Texts*. n.d. Web. 16 May 2015. <http://www.earlychurchtexts.com/public/rufinus_christ_crucified_14_17.htm>.

*sitcom*. n.d. AskDefineBeta. Web. 2 October 2014. <sitcom.askdefinebeta.com>.

Spafford, Horato. "It Is Well With My Soul." Public Domain, 1873.

Speer, Robert E. *Servants of the King*. New York: Young People's Missionary Movement of the United States and Canada, 1909. Print.

Supen, Eric N. *Against All Hope - In Hope Believe*. CreateSpace Independent Publishing Platform, 2010. Print.

*The American Heritage Dictionary of the English Language*. Boston: Houghton Mifflin, 2000. Print.

"The Declaration of Independence: A Transcription." n.d. *National Archives and Records Administration*. Web. 2 October 2014. <http://www.archives.gov/exhibits/charters/declaration_transcript.html>.

*The Other Side of Heaven Taglines*. n.d. Amazon. Web. 14 May 2015. <http://www.imdb.com/title/tt0250371/taglines>.

*The Sound of Music*. Dir. Robert Wise. 1965. Film.

*Visual Bible Alive*. Web. 2 October 2014. <http://www.visualbiblealive.com/resources.php?+category_id=4&encyc_id=594&img_id=29668&action=encyclopedia&frame=divEncyc>.

*What Is Stress?* n.d. The American Institute of Stress. Web. 29 September 2014.

Young, Sarah. *Jesus Today Devotional Journal: Experience Hope Through His Presence*. Thomas Nelson, 2013. Print.

Young, William P. *The Shack: A Novel*. Newbury Park: Windblown Media, 2007. Print.

# My Story

*As Jesus was walking beside the Sea of Galilee, he saw two brothers, Simon called Peter and his brother Andrew. They were casting a net into the lake, for they were fishermen. "Come, follow me," Jesus said, "and I will make you fishers of men." At once they left their nets and followed him.*

**Matthew 4:18-22**

My parents tell me that when I was two years old, sitting in a highchair in a restaurant in Ypsilanti, Michigan, I blurted out to the waitress, "We're having a missionary conference!" Taken aback, the lady looked at me and then at my parents. My parents laughed and explained that our church was having a conference featuring speakers who had given their lives to go overseas and tell people the good news about Jesus Christ. Incredibly, the waitress came to the missions conference and trusted Christ! Like Simon Peter, she was introduced to Christ and, "at once," followed Him.

Obviously the idea of missions made a dramatic impact on my young mind. About the time when other kids are dreaming about becoming doctors, nurses and firemen, I decided to become a missionary and never changed my mind. Every missionary "slideshow" moved me to tears, even as a child.

Much of my motivation came from watching my father. My dad is dedicated to reaching "the next generation." My brothers and I grew up listening to our dad speak to thousands of teenagers about the importance of doing the will of God. My dad's life verse is 1 John 2:17. "And the world passeth away, and the lust thereof: but he that doeth the will of God abideth for ever." The image that has stuck in my memory all these years is of dozens upon dozens of teenagers responding to the invitations to dedicate their lives to doing the will of God.

Many have asked me, "How did you know you were 'called?'" As a little girl, each time I saw kids commit their lives to God my thought was, "*I want God to use me like He's using my dad.*" I wanted to be in the ministry, in the trenches, laying down my life for the Gospel of Jesus Christ. To me there was no greater career than full-time ministry, specifically missions.

Following Christ seemed logical to me growing up. In fact, my name even means "Follower of Christ." When I was five years old, my parents prayed with me and were by my side when I made that all-important decision to place my trust in Jesus Christ alone for salvation and forgiveness of my sins. In AWANA, I memorized countless verses such as, "For all have sinned and fall short of the glory of God," and "While we were still sinners, Christ died for us." It all made sense; I was convinced and willing to follow Christ, even if it meant going to the mission field.

In high school I enjoyed the opportunities to witness and stand up for my beliefs. I also enjoyed being able to choose from five foreign languages. I decided to take German; I loved the funny, harsh sound of it, and my ancestors came from Germany. I remember thinking, *I'll never use this language and I'll probably never see Germany. Only rich people go to Europe.*

In 1996 I entered my freshman year of Bible college. I loved being in a Christian school for the first time and attending chapel every day. In the spring semester, I attended the annual mission's conference. One of the speakers that year had previously been a missionary in Germany. I remember being surprised by this and wondering why Germany would need missionaries. When I thought "mission field," I thought of heat, bugs, mosquito nets, and less-than-reliable electricity. Germany was first-world and the land of the Reformation! Why waste your time there? Why, indeed: I read a quote that day that stated, "Germany, at the heart of Europe, is without a heart for God; 98% is unreached and unsaved. The land of the Reformation is in need of regeneration." That week was life-changing for me. That was the week I prayed and said, "God, if you can use me to make it 97%, I'll go."

The more I thought about Germany in the following years, the more sense it made. As devoted as I was to my missionary "calling," I had always secretly hoped that God wouldn't send me to a hot climate. Germany, I heard, had a "temperate climate." Also, everyone knew that Germany was beautiful—the land of fairy tales.

In the summer of 1998, I decided to go see my future mission field for myself. This is where the rubber started to meet the road. The two-week trip to Bavaria (southern Germany) felt like the longest two weeks of my life. I am convinced that God has a sense of humor, because the temperature was in the 90s the entire time I was there. Germany was breathtakingly beautiful, but I was homesick, lonely, and wanted more than anything to get back home. A week after I got home from Germany, I started my junior year of Bible college. Many asked, "Do you still feel called to Germany?" My answer: "We'll see what God does. I am definitely still praying about it." It wasn't a lie. I was praying about it. I was telling God that I had changed my mind. If you have ever tried to "tell" God something, you know it doesn't work. Within a month or two He used chapel, classes, professors and friends to change my heart and remind me of my passion for the lost and my decision to give up my life for this passion. The most powerful source, other than His Word, that He used to re-kindle my passion was missionary and author Elisabeth Elliot.

I had never heard of Elisabeth Elliot until college (or of Jim Elliot, Nate Saint, Ed McCully, Peter Fleming, or Roger Youderian for that matter). These great missionaries and "heroes of the faith" shaped *my* faith in college. A friend hounded me to read *Passion and Purity*. I was immediately hooked. God used a person I have never met to encourage me more than anyone I *knew* could have. Why? Because she had followed the call of God to the mission field as a single person. She set an example of obedience to the call of God—an achievable one, through the power of the Holy Spirit. "You will receive power [ability, efficiency, might] . . . through the Holy Spirit to be my witnesses" (Acts 1:8).

Elisabeth Elliot did marry, then experienced the murder of her husband two years later, and returned as a missionary to the Huaorani Indians—her husband's murderers. Only the Holy Spirit gives that kind of power, that kind of ability to overcome disappointment, devastation, loss, and overwhelming fear, that strength of spirit to follow God in faith in the midst of seemingly insurmountable obstacles.

I moved to Germany in April of 2004 and have been here 11 years. God has been every bit as faithful to me as he was to Elisabeth Elliot and the scores of others who have chosen to follow Him and fish for men. I praise God for all He has done and is doing in the Land of the Reformation!

Made in the USA
Middletown, DE
16 November 2019